God Does Word Processing Too!

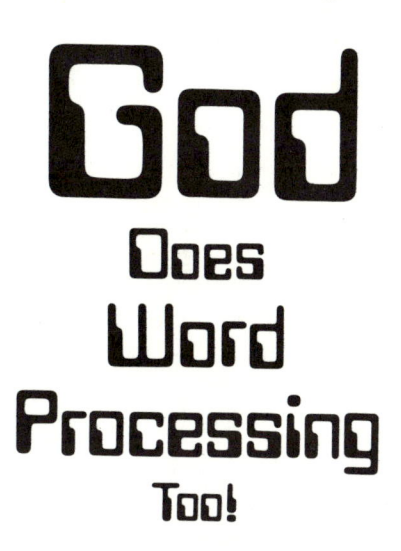

How God Tends to Our Prayers

Joseph Seaborn

Wesley Press
8050 Castleway Drive
P.O. Box 50434
Indianapolis, IN 46250

© Copyright by Wesley Press
All Rights Reserved
Published by Wesley Press
Indianapolis, Indiana 46250
Printed in the United States of America
ISBN: 0-89827-065-0

God
Does
Word
Processing
Too!

Contents

Foreword 7
Introduction 9

Chapter 1
God Hears: Keeping Within Earshot . . . 11
  Does God Ever Plug His Ears? 13
  God Keeps a Hand Handy 23
  Living on the Phone 29

Chapter 2
God Cares: Everything Handled With Care 33
  So Who Needs a Juniper Tree 35
  When the Road Gets Blurry 41
  Trusting God With the Process 45

Chapter 3
God Knows: A World at His Fingertips . . 51
  God Has No Fragment Thoughts 53
  God Has a Mega-Multi-Track Mind . . . 57
  God Is Our "Whether" Forecaster 61
  God Will Move the Dark Glass 65

Chapter 4
God Works: Two Hearts Tugging at One Load 69
  God's Grace Wears Working Clothes . . . 71
  God's Care Runs Deep 75
  God Goes to Where the Hurt Is 81
  God Keeps His Voice Down 85
  Care Changes Things 89

Chapter 5
God Allows: Plenty of Elbow Room . . . 93
  God Is No Snoop 95
  God Lets Us Back Out 101

    God Lives With Loose Ends 105
    God Takes Our Freedom for Real . . . 111
Chapter 6
God Plans: Sticking to the Outline 117
    God Works With a Welter of Motives . . 119
    God Helps the Pieces to Fit 123
    God Makes the Roundabout Way His Way 127
    God Never Second-Guesses Himself . . . 131
Chapter 7
God Helps: Doing a World of Good . . . 135
    God Puts Glory on Our Gum 137
    God Gives Specific Answers to General Prayers 143
    God Watches His Second Hand 145
    God Prefers the Back Door 149
    God Is Working in the Meantime 155

Foreword

This book will not give you the last word on prayer but it certainly will provide a fresh and encompassing look at the matter of conversing with our Heavenly Father. For some, the immediate response to the word "prayer" conjures in one's mind a place, posture or disciplined habit. Throughout this book you will find the recurring theme that prayer is much more – it is an attitude toward life – and a life yielded to God.

Woven throughout the pages are commonly experienced everyday illustrations. A football game, an English teacher's "Sentence Fragments," a weaver's loom, and even a barbershop haircut become helpful avenues to convey this matter of a life of prayer. We are very human in our prayers. Tied to our prayer of faith is a thread of doubt and apprehension. Sometimes our prayers are white flags, last-ditch efforts, or an agonizing plea for mercy. Does God hear those prayers? The author through Scripture assures us God certainly does. The very heart of God is revealed within these pages. You will understand and hopefully respond to the fact that God indeed sees, knows, cares . . . and hurts.

When the prayer is offered up, is there a personal responsibility for the pray-er? Dr. Seaborn gently reminds the reader that God works from a balance of freedom and responsibility. At times praying hands need to be working and willing hands. What about the prayer that God cannot or chooses not to answer? The other side of this balance is God's sovereignty. "If God responded right away to every prayer we send His way He would be neither wise nor Divine" is this author's appropriate reply.

How fresh and vital is your link to heaven? Are you aware of God's presence in creation and in the lives of His creatures? Does your prayer life stir your soul and move you to faith in action? Perhaps this book will be the vehicle to stir your soul to the work of God. I believe you can trust in the Creator's omnipotent hand to respond to your prayers from His heavenly view. ". . . learn to trust the pace of God's process in your life and in the lives of others."

John Maxwell, Pastor
Skyline Wesleyan Church
Lemon Grove, California

Introduction

Have you ever wondered exactly what God does with a prayer? Every day from all around the globe several billion prayers are sent His way. In order to handle that many prayers with the personal attention and love which have become His trademark, God must surely be a fabulous prayer manager. But have you ever wondered how God processes a prayer? Does He trim it down a little? Or rephrase it to line it up with our hearts? Exactly how does God process a prayer?

From our point of view a lot of prayers do not get answered right away and yet we believe that God hears and answers our prayers. If He doesn't, then as one person put it, "Prayer is the nearest thing to nothing that anything can be and still be something." So what's going on with all those prayers that get put on hold? What does God do with them? What is He tending to in the meantime? When the hours stretch into days and the days into years with no apparent reply, what can we learn about the longer turnaround time on our prayers? If we believe deep down that God makes no mistakes in handling our requests, then other factors must be figuring in the process.

What would you do with a prayer? If you were God and were being constantly bombarded with all kinds of prayers, both silly and serious, how would you handle them? Would you occasionally leave one completely unanswered? Would you write off several of them as stupid? Given all the sizes and shapes of prayers, those are not easy questions to answer.

We send God prayers in all sorts of packages. There are round prayers that circle the globe and long prayers that last forever. Solomon's prayer is the longest in the Bible and God answered it (1 Kings 8:23-53). Peter's prayer, "Lord, save me!" is the shortest and God answered it as well. In fact, given the story detail that Peter was drowning, God probably felt a need to get to Peter's right away. But in the end they both got answered. And it is our belief that all prayers get a response. God doesn't misplace anything we send Him. He always processes and replies.

The pages that follow offer lines of thought as to why God may sometimes hold off on the instant response we hope for. No short study like this, nor even a longer one can fully probe the mystery of God's involvement with His children through prayer. No one can say with arrogance that God is or is not responding right away and they know why! However the Bible and Christian experience do point us in several directions for exploring this matter of delayed responses. These chapters pick up on a few of the factors which figure in God's replies to our prayers.

CHAPTER 1

GOD HEARS:
Keeping Within Earshot

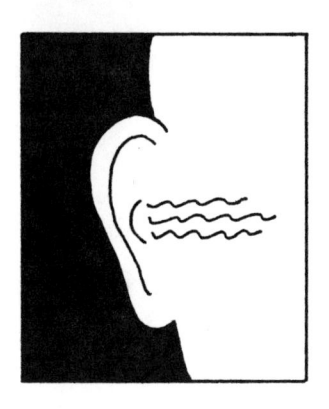

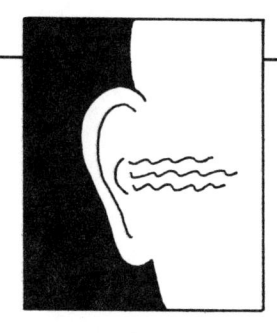

DOES GOD EVER PLUG HIS EARS?

As a young boy growing up in our rural, white, clapboard church, I had definite concerns about God's hearing, especially when Mr. Barrett prayed. Right at the beginning of his prayers, near the "Our Father" part, we guessed that God was picking him up pretty clearly because even those of us sitting nearby in the pews could make out almost every word. But as the prayer grew longer and louder, we figured that God started backing up to see just how far He could back and still hear the prayer. And by the time Mr. Barrett got to the fourfold "Amen," even God himself must have been plugging at least one ear.

The boys who got a kick out of hearing Mr. Bellowing Barrett pray have all grown up now and Mr. Barrett has long since joined the God to whom he talked so loudly, but the vestiges of his manner of praying are still with us. Way down deep in the subconscious of many of us there remains the hunch that to really get God's ear you still need to pitch the voice in a higher key and project it at least to the top of the steeple. The fact is, however, God hears our hearts long before we even open our mouths. He knows what we have need of even before we ask (Matt. 6:8). Neither on God's part nor on ours is there anything that can ever finally be a barrier to prayer. In spite of all the well-known laws to the contrary, prayer cannot be taken out of the public schools. Every day in every school in the world, children and young people can form kneeling pads in their hearts and send their requests and thanks to God. Prayer is like love — legislation can finally neither make it work nor make it fail. The ability of prayer to leap laws and bypass high hurdles is really nothing more than God's way of making sure that matters of the spirit never become dependent on decisions of the flesh. Prayer is strictly a spiritual venture and nothing in the human sphere, whether laws or circumstances, can in the least hinder it if a person genuinely desires to enjoy it. It is part of God's care package to us that we can access His ear without any resistance on His part at all.

In His wise planning, God has never made it necessary for a person to assume any particular position or raise the voice to any special level of loudness in order for him to pray. No position of the body is ever crucial to the growth of our spirit. If it were, somebody somewhere would be excluded on the basis of physical deformity. God would never run His redemptive program with overtones of exclusivism. Truth is, any person anywhere and in any physical position has direct and instant access to the ear of God. Prayer is our 1-800 number to God, no exceptions. As lonely and as discouraged as we may sometimes be, our own mood can never cloud the atmosphere and confuse the signals which link us with God.

Questions about whether it's reachable are not even needed when it comes to God's ear. If God cannot be reached, we may safely conclude that the clutter is not in His ear, but in our souls. A pastor friend included in one of his sermons the story of the man who feared that his wife was losing her hearing and decided to test it out. One day he found her sitting outside in a lounge chair and easing up behind her to within thirty feet he called out firmly,

"Honey, can you hear me?"

No answer. He edged on up to within twenty feet.

"Honey, can you hear me now?"

Steady silence. At ten feet he tried again.

"Honey, can you hear me?"

"Yes," came the reply, "for the third time, yes."

Even when it doesn't seem like it, God hears. His hearing never needs testing, for His ear is never deaf that it cannot hear (Isa. 59:1).

We are people who possess cosmic communication powers. But all too often we stand at the edge of the world and peer off into the sweeps of heaven without taking the leap of heart and visiting there with God. We dally with earthbound hopes when all around us a universe is exploding with life and possibilities far greater than one planet could ever provide. God is everywhere calling us to tear ourselves away from the accumulations of earth which suffer from eternal gravity-bind. He calls us to reach far out and above the sphere of mundane life and by hope to lay hold on truths which the soul spontaneously and correctly calls eternal. The universe only serves as a giant cup to focus our concerns on the ever-hearing ear of God.

All Christians have enjoyed seasons of prayer when words sprang from our mouths in perfect rhythm with our hearts. Occasionally we have known prayer to bubble its way out of our hearts like a geyser of unstoppable love. When prayer flows fresh and free, it's a lot like E. B. White's Model T. He wrote of the times when he cranked the classic old car.

"Often, if the emergency brake hadn't been pulled all the way back, the car advanced on you the instant the first explosion occurred and you would hold it back by leaning your weight against it. I can still feel my old Ford nuzzling me at the curb, as though looking for an apple in my pocket."[1]

But every Christian has also prayed when the sky seemed towering and hushed, as if God had abandoned His listening post. In part that lonely feeling arises in our hearts when we lapse into the old idea that every word we speak to God will receive a clear and prompt response back from Him, that God sends pronto answers to every call. But really, if God responded right away to every prayer we sent His way, He would be neither wise nor divine. The key fault with the instant-answer mentality is that it overlooks the fact that God is God. We are not in control. He is. If God could be cajoled into answering every question, He would be little more than a vast vending machine. We hardly need to even want a push-button God like that. Rather we need a God who picks up every phrase of our prayers but who works on an answer based on His higher heavenly overview and not on the volume of our words. It is for us to deeply and daily believe that God is monitoring every moment of our lives and is always on the lookout for our best interests.

There is no such thing as getting God's attention. When we open a prayer with "Our Father," that in no way compares with what happens when we yell across a crowd for Bob Smith. Surrounded as he is by hundreds of other voices, Bob may well be so absorbed in conversation that several calls are needed before we can catch his eye. But God's name at the start of our call to Him is never helpful in getting His attention. He is always listening. God may have trouble getting *our* attention, but He himself cannot be summoned from afar because He is never away. From His point of view, prayer is never helpful in starting up a conversation. As people we can talk of beginning and ending a conversation with God, but as God sees it, a prayer only means that He is changing His constant monologue to us into a dialogue with us.

Talking with God is a lot like launching a boat into a stream. The stream is always flowing. We are only getting into a movement already in progress. Since God is forever listening and responding, He naturally never misses the beginning or middle or even the ending of our words to Him. From the first word and even further back to the first turn of our heart upward, He is in full attendance because He is right in the same place He was when we closed off our part of the last prayer.

As humans we can't do it very well, but God can listen and talk at the same time. While we are forming phrases to get our message to Him, God can offer intuitive glimpses into His response and even help us in phrasing the prayer. By His Spirit He helps us with groanings which we can hardly utter (Rom. 8:26). He may even help us by answering our questions before we have fully finished the often frustrating task of wording them. It is not that He enjoys interrupting. Since He has the power to vanish the universe with a couple of words, He hardly needs to interrupt us to feel good about throwing His weight around. God often helps us early with the answer to save us the perplexity of precisely framing what we are struggling to say.

He knows that sometimes we know better than to ask what we are asking for. So He steps in to "blush" us with our momentary foolishness. If we ask amiss, He helps us not to fall painfully on our faces by pointing us in another redeeming direction. Nor does God tire of our coming to Him. Unlike the unfair judge who grew weary of the persistent woman, God does not disappear behind the curtains of heaven with His ears covered (Luke 18:1-8). Rather He posts himself permanently nearby, not only to hear our calls for help and questions but, when necessary, to help us with the wording of our concerns as well. The truth ought to be carved in concrete and displayed prominently till the end of time – when it comes to the call of His children, God is all ears.

No New Testament passage more beautifully points out the ongoing care and nearness of God than John 14 and 15. Two truths which sit in this passage rise to tell this message. The first has to do with what Jesus must have been doing physically as He gave this lesson, "I am the vine, you are the branches." The setting for the chapter is the time immediately after the Last Supper as Jesus and His disciples are on that final fatal stroll out to the Garden of Gethsemane where Judas is already stalking. As they walk, the hearts of the disciples are torn by one rending fact. Jesus is leaving. He had been dropping clues for weeks, but now He has told them plainly that He is going to His Father's house very soon. Their minds are in a flurry of fear and grief. No wonder Thomas blurted out the question, "We don't even know where You are going and how can we know the way?"

Right at this point when the disciples are frustrated and hurting all at the same time, their minds staggering with the thoughts of separation, Jesus shares with them a living parable. As they walk, the brilliant moon is beaming down over the hills of Jerusalem. Their path which began in a house back near Mt. Zion winds up through the Temple area where arches and pillars stand out with almost daylight beauty in the night sky. As He walks, fully aware of the pain which is weighing down His disciples' hearts, Jesus motions with a hand up toward one of the archways. Across the arch and down the pillars has been etched a magnificent vine, complete with a large trunk and dozens of tendrils. Clusters of grapes fill the branches.

"Gentlemen," Jesus said, probably pausing a moment or two as He drew their attention to the etchings. "You have been grieving, and rightly so, that I have been talking of separation and of going to My Father's home. But men, I want you to know a great truth that will help your hearts. I want you to look carefully at this lovely carving on this archway. Gentlemen, I too am the vine and you are the branches. Just as surely as the vine and branches here never will be separated, so you and I never finally will be separated. Forever we are going to be tightly grafted together – Me as the vine and you as the branches." Almost instantly the eleven disciples must have felt a large chunk of their anxiety evaporate from their hearts. From that day forward every time they passed by that archway, long after their Master had ascended to heaven, they would have that picture stab them broad awake to the overwhelming truth that Christ was still in them and with them, like a vine is part and parcel of the branches.

Then Jesus repeated a truth which had already been stated earlier at the Last Supper in the evening. "I am going to send you another Comforter who will keep on living with you forever." In the original Greek the word for "another" has a special meaning which must have brought an instant sigh of relief to the hearts if not to the lips of the disciples. There are two major terms for the word "another" in Greek. One is *heteros* which means "another of a different kind." It might be used, for example, by a person forecasting weather to refer to tomorrow as another day, but a day in which the weather is going to be very different from today's. If today has been balmy and pleasant and the forecaster says that tomorrow will be blustery and wintry, we still can say that both are days, but days which are strikingly different.

The other expression, *allos,* also means "another" but it refers to "another of the exact same character" or "another exactly like the present one." If a weather forecaster speaks of an *allos* day, we can go ahead and assume that tomorrow is going to be a repeat of today. Now this is the term which Jesus used with His disciples. "When I go away," He said, "I am going to send you another (*allos*) Comforter who will be with you and care for you in exactly the same way as I have. So don't let your hearts be troubled." Today the Holy Spirit is with us on this earth and His ministry to us is exactly what Jesus would do for and with us if He were still here in person. Just as Jesus listened to His disciples' joys and despairs, so the Holy Spirit listens. Just as Jesus shored up their sagging hearts when the going got rough, so the Holy Spirit remains in our hearts today to be our very present help in time of need.

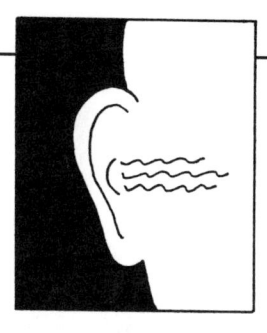

GOD KEEPS A HAND HANDY

The fact that God is with us does not mean that we are removed from the human predicament. While we may no longer earn our living by the sweat of our brow, many of us would quickly acknowledge that we earn our living by the stress of our brow. What once might have been called the "sweat test" might now be called the "stress test." But while we may have thrown away a few of our sweat rags, we still are not further along the road to independence and self-sufficiency. We have only internalized the sweat. The bottom line still reads: We need God's and other peoples' help. We still need God's strength to turn our fret work into faith work. In spite of all our modern gadgets, we only rarely will run into a good solid day of fun. Large portions of life will continue to be times of dependency.

When life catches us coming up on the short end and needing help, God always keeps a person standing nearby to give us help or a word of insight into our need. God never gets down to His last nickel. He always has a hand when He needs one. At just the right time, God grafts a human hand onto His everlasting arm and allows someone once again to be a worker together with God. He fuses the human and divine together and through them lifts our load. As Maria puts it in "The Sound of Music," "When God closes a door, somewhere He opens a window." Our call for help when our own reserves are registering E gets God's energies flowing, for He has promised to be a very present help in time of need (Ps. 46:1).

My friend Della carries with her everywhere she goes a heart pumping with care. When she spots someone whose life has taken a tough turn, she goes to where the hurt is. When our mutual friend, Sarah, lay dying with cancer, Della crowded an already busy schedule with a daily visit to the hospital. Day after day she looked down into Sarah's face, shriveled and gaunt, marked with deep furrows of pain.

"At times," she said, "I would walk down that long corridor in the hospital with waves of anxiety rising in my heart about what I might say to help Sarah today."

One day toward the end of Sarah's life, when she could no longer even force a whisper from her lips, Della climbed into her car and headed for the hospital. As she drove, her mind once again wrestled with the question, "What can I say to Sarah today? What message can I give her that will lift her spirits?"

As she neared the hospital she turned on the

car radio and heard Sandi Patti singing, "We Shall Behold Him." In a flash the Holy Spirit prompted her, "Tell Sarah that. Tell her that we shall behold Him."

Della parked her car and walked into the hospital room that afternoon and without any other introduction, she leaned over close to her dying friend and spoke quietly in her ear. "Sarah, guess what the Holy Spirit gave me to say to you today!"

Sarah could no longer speak, but Della saw a half wink rise from her eyes.

"He told me to tell you that we shall behold Him."

Sarah understood. And in spite of the intense pain she again strained out half a wink. For a quarter of an hour, Della said later, the room was filled with the glory of God. No words were needed. No other signals could have improved on what both of them were feeling together.

"Just the two of us," she said, "enjoying the healing winds of another world."

Several hours later, the phone rang back in Della's office. She picked it up and Sarah was beholding Him.

God takes care of His children. When we occasionally take our turn in the valley of the shadow, even there we must fear no evil, for God has His people standing all around in the wings and He himself is standing by, closer than a brother.

There are days when things go wrong one right after the other and like Martha of New Testament fame, we become discouraged and bogged down with our much serving (Luke 10:40). But God never has to deal with distractions and fatigue. His perfect concentration in all directions keeps Him on top of everything that is happening. As human beings, we are distracted when our attention, focused in one direction, is suddenly drawn in another. But since God thinks in all directions at once, His attention cannot be drawn in another track because for Him there are no unattended directions. To grasp that amazing truth will in itself give our faith a sizable boost forward.

God cannot be taken off guard because He is always on guard. When Judas planted the deadly kiss, God did not leap from His throne and begin pacing the celestial hallways, baffled about what He might do if His Son should be killed. From the beginning of creation, His strategy for salvation was already in mind. His eternal plan was not suddenly thrown into a cauldron of confusion. He was ready.

And God stays ready. He keeps His ear cupped to our call. The splendid silence of a whisper reaches Him in the same half-instant as a high-decibel wail. Our lowest sigh gets to Him as quickly as our loudest cry. When it comes to the call of His children, God never misses a syllable. He listens closely to a five-year-old mumble the prayer He has heard millions of times, "Now I lay me down to sleep." He hears a construction worker's prayer over the noise of a jackhammer. The housewife working in the solitude of her kitchen gets through instantly. A banker, as her fingers fly across the face of a calculator, has split-second access. No noisy gongs or deafening silences keep our concerns from reaching the all-hearing ear of God.

Like Della and Sarah, you and I run into pockets of life where twinges of pain or personal clutter seem to have jammed God's reception. Heaven seems as remote as a dim star on a hazy night. From our point of view, we have lost the bubbly certainty that God is even listening. But God wants us to know deep down that He never turns His ears from our pleas. On days when our interruptions are only broken by further interruptions, He assures us that He is standing by to hand us a heaping helping of His peace. Our minds, He promises, will be kept in perfect peace as they are able to stay focused on Him (Isa. 26:3). God promises His all-out twenty-four-hour presence and simply asks that as much as possible we promise Him ours as well.

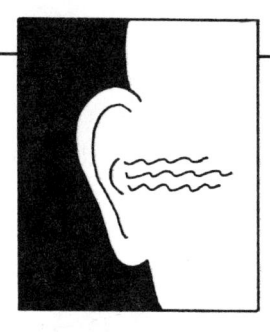

LIVING ON THE PHONE

While browsing in a family bookstore, I overheard a little boy who looked to be about seven years old doing a delightful verbal number on his father. His father stood there calmly thumbing randomly through a thick volume. But right underneath that book and peeking over the edge was his son. Apparently I had missed a good deal of the prior conversation, but I did enjoy eavesdropping as the little chap moved in for the kill. His request, heavy with formality, amused me.

"Father," he appeared to use the word in much the same way my father used to use the word "son" just before a major corrective session. "Father, did you know that I desire to have this book?"

He shoved a thin book on horses over his head up to his father. His father shuffled his feet and kept on turning the pages in the bigger volume. Not a sound.

"Father," he came at his dad again, "do you know that I am going to stand here until I wear you down?"

Not too shabby an attack for a seven-year-old, I thought. Lots of persuasion and amateur psychology working in those words. According to my watch it took him about five minutes, but he got his book. As I left the store I glanced back one more time. The little boy was standing beside the cash register patting his book and grinning a big winner's smile up toward his father.

That story may not cut it as a model for family relations, but in the realm of faith it is an analogy with both a weak and strong point. The weak one is that God cannot be argued down. He is not impressed with our clever rebuttals and witty logic. If He knows what we have need of even before we ask, a try at mental manipulation is not going to miscue His higher wisdom concerning our need. God can't be wheedled into anything.

We may run away from God and search out substitute fathers to get us what we want. But if God knows we really need a thing, if it really blends in with our long-range good, He does not need our little run at persuasion. If we genuinely need it, He has already decided to get it for us before we ever peek over the edge of His book to ask for it (Isa. 65:24).

This bookstore incident reveals a helpful truth as well. God wants us to ask. He lets us ask to train us in the virtue of asking, of turning to Him as our regular helper.

One of the most puzzling questions in the practice of prayer has to do with the need to keep up the asking. God encourages us to keep saying our prayers, not because of His forgetfulness, but in order to let us make sure that we are asking for what we really want. In Luke 18, Christ praises a woman who pressed on into the presence of the judge, requesting *ad nauseam* until the judge granted her request. And Christ cites her persistence as a model for prayer. We are to keep saying it to sustain it in our own hearts. One fact blazes with clearness. The repetition of her request did not reflect on the memory of the judge. On the contrary, he was downright annoyed with the boring redundancy of the woman's request. What stands out in this passage like a thriving tree in a desert is that the woman, by vowing to stop at nothing in her quest, showed beyond question that she was serious about her case. She probably did not phrase her petition the same way each time, but the judge could not mistake it that she meant business.

In that ironic two-verse couplet, Jesus tells His disciples, "Do not be like them (hypocrites), for your Father knows what you need before you ask Him. This is how you should pray:" (Matt. 6:8-9a). Well, if God knows, doesn't He mock us by telling us to ask? No, God knows that the habit of asking and therefore talking to Him is as valuable as a specific reply. God does not always directly give us the answer we are seeking. Sometimes He gives us something even better – himself. One of the best ways He can give us himself is by spending time listening to our questions. We don't always need God to answer our questions, we often need Him to be himself the answer to our questions.

Sometimes what we interpret as God thumbing through a heavenly book to avoid us is really Him waiting and listening so that we can sell our own heart on the rightness of our prayer, that our meaning closely parallels our words. When we come up with the right request, the best one for us, His answer will be so close to the one we desired that we will stand back amazed and call it a definite answer to prayer.

Phrasing a prayer through our lips is several times easier than phrasing it truly from our hearts. Terms like "if God wills," "at any cost," and "for my highest good" find easy exit from the mouth, but the heart releases them much more slowly. And it is right here at this point where God exercises His long-winded patience. When God made us with free wills, He meant it. When He put the ability to decide into a lump of clay, He did it on purpose. And because of that, God often winds up having to wait for the free persons He has made to truly want His will. This poem, though short, still requires two readings to make sense. But it does make sense.

> *If any wills to do God's will,*
> *Then to will is well.*
> *For he who wills to do God's will,*
> *Within God's will will dwell.*

God can wait a long time for us to will to do His will. But when we do, when we finally set our hearts to do His desire, He bursts into our lives with a sense of new assurance and quiet peace. God never fails to respond to a consecrated prayer. When in our deepest hearts our will becomes His will, we revel in a higher awareness of His nearness than ever before, and any specific answers which He chooses to send along are just divine icing on an already delicious cake.

CHAPTER
2

GOD CARES:
Everything Handled With Care

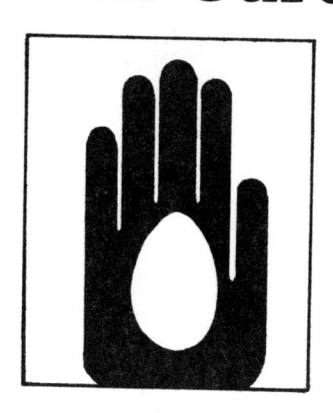

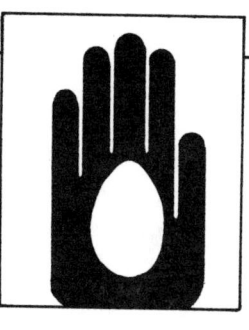

SO WHO NEEDS A JUNIPER TREE?

Anyone who has ever deeply linked their heart and hands with the pain of a friend knows that absorbing care costs a lot of personal energy. Compassion drains off precious time and natural energy. Any thinking person will argue with vigor that it is a noble thing to do. But the same thinker will also have to readily admit that genuine caring takes its toll. My close friend Bonnie was expressing a very natural response to compassion fatigue in the letter she wrote concerning her father. She wrote of staying at his bedside into the early morning hours, of attempting to carry on conversation with a man whose mental faculties were fading rapidly, and of enduring the exhaustion of running back and forth between work and family and father. After several lines in which she explained his frustrating battle with Alzheimer's disease, she added these words, "I catch myself praying for him to die and it scares me so badly that I wonder if that very prayer is sinful. I love my father but I am really struggling with the thought that death might be the best for all of us."

In a letter of response I made two brief points. First, death is one of God's ways of bringing healing. Though God can give one of several responses, for people who have lived long and well it ought to be counted a lovely miracle when He chooses the healing of death. And second, sometimes our prayers which seem so harsh and cruel are really only deep reflections of our own emotional tiredness. Even people of high energy can run down, their reasoning can be thrown off balance, and patterns of unthinking behavior may result. Accept these things, for they are part of being yourself and God loves you for who you are. God fully understands that with His people the cutting edge of care can dull.

The rub comes when we let the fact that human beings tire and run down spill over into our understanding of God – that He too somehow loses heart and wavers from His initial intense concern. Human energy is a limited commodity. But God's first and last levels of concern are the same. His strong regard for our needs never fades. The trudge of time never causes it to diminish. God keeps giving out His love with the same ease on the twentieth day and the two hundredth day as He did when the need first arose.

The ability of God to give with sustained and undiminished abandon is difficult to keep in mind when every human model we see around us is regularly being drained of energy and in constant need of refreshment. We almost need an eraser for the mind to correctly convince ourselves that God gives and gives and gives again without ever a hint of slacking off.

Eight hundred and seventy years before Christ, God called a man of Israel by the name of Elijah to do a series of marvelous miracles in order to show that God alone was truly God. Moving back and forth through the land with all the panache and flourish of a lion tamer, Elijah squelched God's enemies and chased out intruders. One afternoon on Mt. Carmel after a sixty-three-word prayer and with the God of heaven to back him up, Elijah scored a direct hit on Baal worship in the countryside, and 850 prophets of this god of fire lay dead in the scorching sands. That day on Mt. Carmel one man plus God took on an army and won the contest hands down.

But give him a couple of days and let him overhear the rumor that Ahab and Jezebel, king and queen of Samaria, are out to take his life, and Elijah is on the road and running for his life. Several days and 120 miles later he finds himself lying under a juniper tree praying a prayer which is soaked with defeat, "Oh God, let me die." Can you believe it? The same prophet who had seen a tiny cloud the size of a man's hand and had predicted a cloudburst based on that scant evidence is now lying in the pity puddle of discouragement, his faith low, his spirit whipped.

And there will be times when life's pressures will come with the pace of a freeway at rush hour. Chores will crunch in bumper to bumper. If in times like that you could sprout juniper trees you would probably need to plant them as close together as parking meters on main street. During life's down moments, it takes a very robust and zesty faith to remember that while God needs no juniper tree, He is always in search of people lying under them. He is never subject to a mood of despair or a dark night of the soul. He continues His full-time full-tilt ministry to each of us without a single second of rest or even a need for it.

Sure God lets His children do lots of things for themselves, but at every stage along the way, He promises and sends His help. It is a major mistake to think that when God rested after six days of creation that He turned away from His creation. It is better to say that He simply set himself to another phase of His steady creative work.

Two words used in the creation accounts in Genesis suggest this ongoing work of God. One of the terms is *bara*. It means to create something out of nothing, to fill empty space with things and people. God only needed six days to create in the *bara* sense. But the other word, *yatsar,* has been part of His lifestyle since day seven of world history. *Yatsar* refers to God working with people and things which He has earlier created from nothing, to forming and fashioning them into His ideas of beauty. It suggests that God continually engages himself in the ongoing life of His people and His world. In terms of time, God's greatest creative work has been occurring since the end of the first six days.

It is also delightful to remember the truth that after the initial six days of creation God did not need to rest for himself. Creation didn't tax Him. He probably didn't even notice the labor part, absorbed as He was with the finished product. He only rested to give us a model for how to do it. But immediately after He showed us the way to rest, He set himself to the lifelong process of co-creating with the people whom He had made. He holds a year-round ticket to all of our lives and He attends all that we do in order to offer His help. We sometimes vacuum up this down-home desire of God to help and we cover it up with the carpet of ornate theology. But a lot of what terms like "sovereignty" and "immanence" mean, is that God enjoys our company. He never ever tires of hearing and helping us. The quality of His giving is never strained.

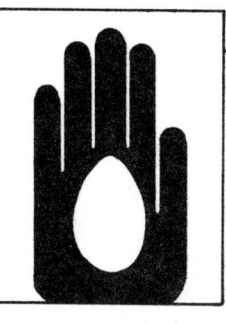

WHEN THE ROAD GETS BLURRY

Very few experiences in life can compare with that of having to drive in the wee hours of the morning when you are so sleepy that your eyes are rolling and wobbling like two satellites on the verge of falling from orbit and your hands are so numb that you don't know if that odd sensation is the steering wheel or just the other hand gone unconscious.

On a vacation several years ago, my in-laws, a sister-in-law and my wife and I set out one night at 6:00 p.m. to cross the state of Texas by interstate. The station wagon in which the five of us rode was packed up to the ceiling on both sides with just enough clear space for the view through the rearview mirror to be legal. Items which had originally filled the illegal space had been carefully placed under the seats so that at sudden stops, they could roll out and chisel bruise marks on our heels. My father-in-law, apparently unhappy with the prospects of having to sit with two other people in the front seat, had carved out a space behind the third seat next to the automatic rear window. Until he went to sleep he kept describing in more detail than any of the rest of us cared to hear the sights in his view straight up. A skein of yarn occupied one rider. The *Reader's Digest* held a third, and the fourth made a noble attempt at going to sleep, distracted of course by the running commentary on power lines and tree limbs arising from near the rear window.

By 10:00 p.m., however, everything had ceased. The knitting, the reading, the commentary – everything, that is, except my driving. And there I sat. For three, four, five hours I sat. Not a hotel within a light-year. Those white and yellow lines in the center of the highway had long since become an oblong off-white blur. As long as I kept the car astraddle of the blur I figured at least I would stay a reasonable distance from the ditch. I tried to stay awake by rolling down the window and sticking my head out with my mouth open. Due to the sudden surprise of a sixty-mile-an-hour wind, my eyelids began flapping around like oversized flip-flops which you have to grip with your toes to keep on your feet. I vowed that the first hotel that turned up would be ours, no matter if it were rat-infested or two hundred dollars per night. I'd stick it on the American Express card before anybody else could get awake enough to stop me. Have you ever noticed that money is no object when you are that close to death?

Finally, after a time that ran a close second to eternity and enough coffee from the canteen to float the same battleship which Winston Churchill could have floated with his bourbon, I spotted a hotel sign and zigzagged toward it like one would a lifeline. What the rest of the crew did, I can't distinctly remember. My hunch is that when my father-in-law woke up, he must have thought that we had hit an awfully long stretch of road without powerlines. If I had been awake I would have agreed.

Every Christian has known times in the long stretches of life when God seems so far away that He may as well be off working with another world, when life has gathered in with fury and pain, and strain marks our days. It is not always easy in times like that to form the words from our hearts, "I believe in God the Father almighty. . . ." In fact for many Christians there are days when they are genuinely frustrated about the question of whether or not God even cares. We could scorch the air with statements we have heard people make as they shook a mental fist at God for not moving in to help them in the time and way they chose.

God knows about anger and frustration. Being as big as He is, God becomes an easy target for angry outbursts and challenges. It's one of the occupational hazards of being God. The good news is, God can handle our concerns. When He goes to His mailbox to see what messages His world has sent that day, He knows very well that some of the letters will be so hot that they should have been written on asbestos paper. He also knows that many of the messages will be glad thanks for His help in a local setting. A portion of the communications will be from sincere Christians who have an honest question. It seems out of character to think of Christians yelling and screaming at God, but honest questions which are couched in a searching faith are very much in order with Him.

One of my seminary professors told of a lady in his congregation who called him one day and before he could finish his hello, she was scalding him about a sentence in his Sunday sermon which she thought was aimed at her. Just as she was pouring it on with her white-hot best and relishing the attack, he hung up on her. In seconds his phone rang again.

"I'll have you know, dear Pastor, you will not hang up on me!" He said the tone in her voice sounded as if she meant it.

"Oh yes, I will," he shot back, "and I'll be most happy to do it again unless you are willing to give me at least half the time to talk."

I'm pretty sure that God doesn't retort with the blunt boldness of the pastor, but there must be times when people blather on in unreasonable anger, unwilling to listen, when God, if He were human, would certainly clobber the daylights out of them. But He doesn't. His long-winded patience and His awesome sense of who He is prevents Him from needing to defend himself. In fact He must endure the difficult awareness that free moral persons who thrash out at Him are really behaving in a way that will have far more serious impact on them than on Him.

How much better to start our quest and questions with faith in God that His way is the best way and then give ourselves to searching out as much as we can of the mystery through which we are passing. What we may discover is that there is something in the nature of faith which in itself helps us with our answers.

TRUSTING GOD WITH THE PROCESS

Bob's a friend of mine. Due to company cuts, he found himself out of a job. As a father of three and with his wife working, he felt the urgent need to find new work as soon as possible. For three full weeks, morning and night, he spent his time knocking on company doors, filling out applications and waiting. One job would look promising but the wages would be quite low. Another interview would ring clear. He'd tell his wife he was pretty sure he'd land this job and bang, the door would slam again.

After three weeks of applying, praying and hoping, he finally met a man in the same business as he had worked before, and by the end of the day Bob was hired. The pay was excellent, working conditions ideal – a perfect fit. The family celebrated with a trip to a fancy restaurant.

It struck Bob like a boulder two days later when the new manager walked into his office and said, "I'm sorry, Bob, you're fired." Bob was devastated. It took him several days to absorb the blow of being treated so rudely. He learned a week later that the man had found out he was a Christian. That was the strike against him. In that company most of the money was made by crooked means.

Bob experienced what is common to all of us. Feelings figure big in human experience. Over time our moods run the whole range from elation to depression, from what John Bunyan calls the "icy river" to Cowman's "streams in the desert." Because we are neither disembodied spirits nor soulless bodies, but soul and body bound in one bundle of life, our bodies are affected by our spirits and the other way around. They catch each other's sicknesses and share each other's health. Comments, careless comments, made by otherwise charming people, often catch us off guard and push our spirits even further into despair. But we will have more than one occasion to meet several of God's dear children otherwise known as the oddly godly, so we may as well be ready for them.

That's why it's necessary to remember that God is concerned with helping us, that life is a process and not a single point. If we try to live life taking any single point of emotion as representative of the whole thing, we will struggle with a faith which is as fickle as a wind sock. But if we can see that God's care is spread out across the process of our lives, we will not be nearly as likely to get blown over by the hostile winds of a single storm.

Emotions are valuable. In assembling people, God created emotions and meshed them with the rest of our parts to form His highest created being.

Our emotional patterns can influence our motivation. Emotions can set off the spark of our desires which draw us toward our goals. And like fuel, emotions may run low and cause motivation to lag. But a full tank of happy feeling brings a surging urge to get up and get moving. We should not even attempt to air-condition our emotions, always trying to be cool, calm and detached. We ought to feel and feel strongly, but we must also be careful not to tie our feelings and faith to the same barometer.

Although we are often apt to equate low feeling with low faith, thankfully Christian faith does not yo-yo with our feelings. Like Bob when he was hired and fired within a few days' time, many of us as Christians with a strong faith in Christ find our feelings running up and down the emotional range. Our feeling gauge reflects both weal and woe, crests and troughs, and both are commonplace in the human experience. Miscellaneous moods belong to the stuff of life. The key to successful faith living is to trust God in the process of life instead of judging God's direct involvement at any single point along the way. The Bible notes that God works all things together for our good. Any single event may not in itself be particularly good, but if we are patient with God's giving process, all things, even unpleasant things, will be molded and shaped so as to improve us.

In one of his unguarded moments Peter said a thing so characteristic of him. Sequestered on a mountain with several friends and Jesus, he announced his wish to locate permanently. But if Christ had granted his wish, Peter probably would have been the first to grumble about the dull solitude of the mountaintop. Nobody faults Peter for letting go in a moment of enthusiasm, reveling on the peak with his friends. An occasional outburst of glowing Christian exuberance expands the spiritual lungs. But for Christians, isolated mountaintop moods can spell danger if we attempt to stake out a little high spot and settle down. The attitude of the little rock must not be ours.

> *I wish I was a little rock*
> *A-sittin' on the hill.*
> *I wouldn't do a single thing*
> *But just keep sittin' still.*

Not only would we find the sustained emotional high discontenting, but we would miss completely the purpose for which intense Christian experience is designed — service. What stirs the soul and goes no farther, damages the character. The value of happy moments with the Master is conserved only as feeling feeds into duty. Divine stirrings in our emotions are only perishable luxuries, unless we bring the experience down close-range to people in the plain of everyday toil and testing and tell them all that we have seen and heard. It is the show and tell in the valley that God also wants to work together for our good.

The key truth headlined in Romans 8:28 is that God can be trusted to handle the process, the unfolding of our lives. Instead of hinging our hopes to a high mood or a single stroke of success, we are encouraged to bank our faith in the character of God. As our faith in God grows, we show less and less tendency to beat the air aimlessly. We discover that God has more to do with us than to just bring us to salvation. He wants to keep us company and to offer His help along the way.

In several areas of northern Michigan canoe racing is a popular sport. A few months ago I took out a couple of hours to drive over to a canoe race near Traverse City. I selected a spot on the bank which another bystander said was the whitest part of the rapids. Even with my amateur eye and nobody else close enough to offer color commentary on what was really happening between the men and their rapids, I drew several novice conclusions. One poor fellow came charging down the river, arms flailing, oar swinging wildly as he tried to stay upright. I guessed that he was using about the same precision of arm and hand movements which one would use to wield a flyswatter in a room buzzing with seventy flies. Slap! Poke! Jab! Slam! Splat! He whacked at rocks five feet to the left and right of the canoe and a couple of times at rocks already well behind him. Low hanging limbs he sheared off with the oar. My mind ran to Moses who struck the rock to produce water. My hunch was that if Moses had struck the rock hoping for a spigot-size flow of water, this fellow had his heart set on a local flood!

To add to the amusement, he was followed in the contest by what looked to me to be an expert. This man came bobbing down the stream in his yellow and brown canoe. His run required a whole new set of adjectives. Poised, graceful, gentle, rhythmic. Instead of fighting the water he seemed to be able at just the right moment to turn its power to his purpose. A little oar tap on the water here, a gentle pirouette of the body there and he had come and gone so gently that I wondered if the water had suddenly grown calm. It hadn't. He won.

As our faith in Christ matures, we learn more and more that slapping and jerking in the twists and turns of life is not where it's at. We so readily claw at life's irritations and gripe at its bends before we remember that God's power is underneath us and

His hand is poised to guide us. The lesson of the expert canoeist is slow in coming, but it is worth the wait. God can be trusted to help us in the processes of life.

CHAPTER

3

GOD KNOWS:

A World At His Fingertips

GOD HAS NO FRAGMENT THOUGHTS

When I was in the tenth grade my teacher, Mr. Newton, got into a bad habit of writing the unsightly letters "SF" at various places in my composition papers. Not only did it ruin the aesthetic appeal of the paper, it also needled my pride. But Mr. Newton made no bones about it, he had a marked dislike for "Sentence Fragments." Several of us students were convinced that he could sense one coming up, down the page. Then when he passed back the papers he would give his moth-eaten speech, "Now students," he would start with his eyebrows lowering to match his tone, "sentence fragments lead to confusion and you can never precisely state a confused idea."

And we would join together as a class in denouncing sentence fragments as one of the great scourges of the human family, the bubonic plague of modern composition. At least we did so until the next composition paper deadline.

God must often observe our thought processes and realize that we too are thinking and praying in thought fragments. While to us it may seem that we have grasped the full sweep of a great truth or that we are praying with clear and complete insight into all the issues, God in His higher wisdom knows that we have latched on to only bits and pieces of the truth. Paul is exploring this very idea in 1 Corinthians 2:1-8. In a paragraph contrasting human and divine wisdom, he declares that if the leaders of Jesus' day had really known who Christ was and what He was doing here, they would not have crucified Him, the Lord of glory. In their limited knowledge, influenced by Satan's scheming, they committed a crime which a higher and holier knowledge would have prevented.

The fact of our partial thinking is evidenced regularly in the daily round. Watch the head coach on the sidelines during a football game. A phone plugged into his ear keeps him in touch with three or four coaches perched high above the field. Another half dozen people huddle around him as his brain trust on the field. The offensive coach, defensive coach and any number of players are standing by ready to offer their views on the best playing strategies. The very presence of so many paid observers hints of the partial nature of any of their observations alone.

Another more internal bit of evidence that contrasts our mind with God's is the fact that even in our peak mental periods, we are never able to completely unify all the bits of truth which we know into one coherent fully meshed system. We may have a reasonable handle on the truths of God's otherness from us, His transcendence, and His nearness to us, His immanence. But to fully figure out how He can be both the sovereign God beyond to whom we pray and the present God within who gives us strength, catches the human mind leaping back and forth with more or less emphasis on God's nearness or farness depending on our need. Try as hard as you will at weaving these two clear biblical truths into a greater whole and you will find your mind annoyed by a sense of twoness; God is other, God is here. Despite trying to chase out the notion of two truths, the duality keeps muscling in to prevent our full resolution into one.

What's more, if we linger too long in the area of these two truths, we will find them being joined by a number of their relatives, all of whom are clamoring with good reason to belong to our attempts at mental merger. And this very tendency to break truth into smaller and more manageable segments tells us in a way often frustrating that we live with limited minds. Plus, even fragment thoughts are crushed a little as our mind grasps them. To even try to lift our thoughts to God's level is probably a little like trying to play Handel's "Messiah" on a set of spoons. The universe simply will not fit all at once into a human mind.

But God does not struggle with fragment thinking. He lays hold of all thoughts at once and complete. All the issues surrounding a situation are focused as clearly as if He were tending to one item alone. Nobody will ever be able to write "SF" on God's thought patterns. If several of the teachings in the Bible appear partial, they are given in that manner as a concession to the human mind and not as a need on the part of God. God knows. His full knowledge of every person at all times and under every condition is one of the tremendously consoling certainties of the Christian faith. Job was more correct than either he or we will ever know – God knows the way that we take (Job 23:10).

GOD HAS A MEGA-MULTI-TRACK MIND

When Isaiah mentioned that God's thoughts are higher than ours, he was onto something big (Isa. 55:9). To put it a bit more pointedly, God can just plain out-think us. God, for example, always thinks about our problem and its solution at the same time. Without using up a single extra click on the clock, He can collapse our futures and our presents and pasts into a single divine snapshot, framing all three time segments in a single image. He easily compresses a thousand years into a day or less. God enjoys a memory of the future just as easily as He has premonitions of the past. Then and now and someday all get folded into His eternal now.

In His one mighty person, God brackets both ends of history and like a giant bellows, squeezes yesterdays so closely to tomorrows that for Him they both become the brimming instant of the now. God never gets stuck in time lock. Before we were, He was, and already He lives beyond our futures waiting for us to arrive. Paul was thinking in just this neighborhood when he borrowed the concept in a capsule, "For in him we live, and move, and have our being" (Acts 17:28).

The fact that God has higher thoughts than ours really has nothing to do with altitude. Just as the claim that God's thoughts are long thoughts has nothing to do with miles or even light years. Isaiah is simply dealing with the fact that words too fall short of the glory of God. Whatever thoughts we offer to God in prayer are strengthened as His thoughts run to meet ours. But not only does God's mind move in tandem with ours to guide and guard like a father leading his child on a trainer bicycle, God's mind also marches out ahead of ours, charting ideal turns and scouting out the mental mine fields. When we pray to be led around and safely by temptation, we are only asking God to apply to our lives data which He has already filed. He never barges in and overrides our free minds, but if we ask His help, we are tapping into the supreme information network in which information float time is determined for the most part by how long it takes us to ask.

God's is a mega-track mind. To do all He has to do, it would have to be. When we label a person as having a one-track mind, we are not far from the truth. Even when our minds are running at full tilt, we are never able to think clearly about more than one thing at a time. One strand of thought at a time is our top and bottom limit. In our most alert hours the maximum number of items that we can contemplate at any given instant is one. And even on that one thought alone, our mind is still holding it at a level several spheres below the infinite and natural flow of the mind of God.

On the other hand, God's eternal mind, like an unending line of strings on a loom, holds every thought in equal awareness at all times. Nor can God ever think less than every thought. At no time does a single strand get lost in the shuffle of the shuttle. God has no need to tie a knot in His memory, because He never breaks thought. In His complete consciousness of everything at all times, He does not need to focus on this or that global concern because He is always equally and fully aware of every thought, word and deed of everyone everywhere. Nothing we can ever do makes God know more or less about us.

For twenty years my father stood day after day over a thousand strands of thread as they spun their way along a series of shuttles and cylinders on their way from raw cotton to bolts of beautiful cloth. Hour by hour he scanned up and down the full spectrum of threads searching for a frayed section or a break, ready to clip out the faulty fragment and to tie a deft weaver's knot to send the solid strand securely on its way. Sometimes when several strands were defective, Dad had to briefly stop the loom in order to clip and tie several repair knots. Then it was back to power and on and on.

Unlike Dad at the shuttle, God never needs to stop His thought flow to mend or to repair. No thought ever slips. No idea ever frays. No notion ever fragments the perfect movement of His mind. He carries all His thoughts in sure and rhythmic flow. And every thought in the minds of the billions of people on earth is always transparent and open unto Him with whom we have to do (Heb. 4:13).

For the people of God that fact brings welcome relief. Alert as He is to all of life, God is closely monitoring our ways so that when we misstep spiritually He stands immediately by to reroute our direction and to rekindle our love.

GOD IS OUR "WHETHER" FORECASTER

Two truths about God are all the more striking when they are taken together. The first is that God is infinite and unbounded, equally filling vast light-years of space and thimble-size crannies. The second is, God knows His creation in detail. For human beings these two teachings require a trade-off. The more we know in general, the less we can know in particular. But God is equally versed at both ends of the continuum.

We often wonder why God created such a gigantic universe. Why did He span out distances so far that light grows old just traveling between them? As one person jested, the factory seems way too large for such a small product as man. But maybe not. Perhaps to God the universe is not big at all. When you talk about God and His hugeness, frankly the universe, however roomy, is rather small. Take a working analogy. Compared to the unbounded God, let's say that our universe weighed in at about the size of a BB. If you take a tiny BB, or place it on the ground at your feet, peer down at it and call it the universe, that at least gets the mind moving in the right direction concerning God's perspective. But there is another step which would bring us even closer to reality. If you looked at that same BB and knew that five billion plus persons lived there and for any one of them you could rattle off the number of molecules in their body and the number of hairs on their skin, you would be getting nearer to a sense of the regular conditions under which God lives.

Therefore, because of His giant overview and His detailed inner view, God knows whether this or that option would be better for us. We never help our cause by nodding God off when He disagrees with us. Toward the end of every prayer, we ought to insert a phrase which must always mark the attitude of our heart: Thy will be done. There are a couple of smart reasons for working this phrase in. First, it stands as a constant reminder that even when our mind is functioning at its maximum output, it still may miss a great deal of all that is involved in the issues about which we are praying. Asking God's will is telling God that if our request falls short on common sense, go ahead and scratch it. And second, if the direction of our request makes good sense in the short run, we need to let God check it for the long haul. If His longer view spots a consequence which we have not foreseen, we pray wisely and well if we ask Him to have it His way.

Father does know best. As the supreme "imagineer" God can sort through all the options to see which will place us at greatest advantage. With His uncanny and unfailing knack for testing out any one of several options before it is chosen, it only stands to reason that when our roads diverge in a yellow wood, we only benefit by consulting with the One who sees the divergence from the other end.

For God creativity is the joy of being asked to share knowledge and lend suggestions which He already knows to be most helpful. Strictly speaking, God will not have a new thought today that He has never had before. His mind is not in evolution. His thoughts are not in process. Everything that He will ever know He already knows and everything He ever knew at the beginning is identical with everything He will know at the end. His mind has never surprised Him by turning over a brand-new idea and never will.

Just spading around the outer edges of such a majestic mind like that is elevating. And since His knowledge of my particular future is always being exercised for my good, my confidence level in His care can take a giant step forward as I get a clearer view of His mental agility ability. His mastery of my options coupled with His commitment to my highest good makes my decision to go with His "picks" the wisest and safest move of all.

GOD WILL MOVE THE DARK GLASS

There probably was a time long ago when one brilliant man or woman could hold in memory the sum total of human knowledge. But today we can only know a pinch of the whole. Such restricted human knowledge makes it easy to assume that God's knowledge too has been squeezed into one specialized sphere. But that isn't true. God is not hemmed in by a cocoon of confined knowledge. God holds all knowledge and all points of view of that knowledge always in mind.

As people we have a fragile foothold on the mountain of information in our world. Yet with our limited awareness, we hurry to make decisions which often cost us plenty because we do not know enough. We grab pieces of reality and run off to lord it over areas of life about which we know next to nothing.

Then when our decisions collapse in failure around us, we wonder why God did it to us. It would be nearer to reality to simply acknowledge that our view of life through the dark glass will every now and then, in spite of all we can do, lead to a few awkward moments. Sin is very much with us, and poor decisions as well as indecision are the direct result of it.

Suppose we had been born and had grown up all of our lives under a fog so thick that the farthest anyone had ever seen was twenty-five feet. Such a cramped perspective would change our perception of daily life. Football fields would have to be shorter so that fans would not have to be constantly shuffling back and forth in the stands to see the game. Skyscrapers would run up a couple of stories and disappear. Or maybe our tallest skyscrapers would be two-story. The term "landscape" would have to be shrunk down to a small backyard. In planning for a hike, one could not visually judge distances between hills. At the peak of a mountain there would be no sense of the valley below. Every action in our visual space would be collapsed to the confines of a half-dome fifty feet wide.

And then suppose that one morning we awoke to discover that someone had pulled back the covers, that the fog had evaporated, and in one incredible magnifying moment, we had multiplied our visible world fifty times. The once claustrophobic closeness of the low vault had given way to brilliant unfurled stretches of openness and sky. What a terrific day it would be to collect all the daily newspapers to see what pictures they would show and what stories they would tell.

Now we know in part, declares Paul, but in that great day when heaven becomes ours we shall know face to face (1 Cor. 13:12). Some day the cover will in fact be folded back. But even in that grand day when our minds shall take a higher road and know reams more than they know now, we shall be scratching only a dent on the surface of our potential knowledge of God. Fitted with heaven's new capabilities, yes, but greater, fitted with new sensors for learning even more about the majesty of God. No matter how far we go in comprehending God's greatness, the ever-unfolding process will always be like trying to measure the circumference of the earth with a yardstick. The sudden transition from our abilities to know in this world, to our capacity for knowing in the next, will undoubtedly seem like we have gone from pitch darkness into a marvelous new light. The sudden flourish of new scenes and senses will remind us again that we are children of Him who said, "Behold I keep on making all things new" (Rev. 21:5).

CHAPTER 4

GOD WORKS:
Two Hearts Tugging At One Load

GOD'S GRACE WEARS WORKING CLOTHES

It was on an ordinary afternoon that Christ hung silhouetted against the drab sky on top of a skull-shaped hill. The sky was menacing and angry. His blood that trickled over the edge of the axe-hewn wood formed tiny puddles as it dropped in gentle rhythms to the rocky ground below. Fresh-picked thorns sunk to the skull through the soft skin crowning His head. And it is this picture more than any other in history which tells us that God relates to our pits of pain because He's been there. It would have taken a stout stomach for anyone to have looked life in the face on crucifixion day and declare that God really cares. But the cross was only the visible part of the story. The unseen part which made the difference was the Father hovering so near to His Son that Jesus only had to whisper to talk to Him. If ever you could argue that God compressed himself for one intense moment of communication, the cross would surely be the case in point.

It is a mark of strained nonsense to argue that God the Father sat far off and unfeelingly by, while God the Son bled His heart out for the human family. Grace argues against that. Our theology has long argued that there is only one God. Since that is true, then at the crucifixion too there was only one God and that God felt pain. Each pound of the hammer sent shock waves of agony straight into the heart of God.

It is not from Scripture, but from an old Greek concept that we get the notion that God cannot suffer. The Bible notes that He is touched with the feeling of our weaknesses (Heb. 4:15). It says that God was genuinely grieved when He saw His human creation foul up so badly (Gen. 6:6). This is not God second-guessing himself, but rather God willing to identify fully, even to the point of personal heartache, with the free human beings whom He created.

Far from denying the wonder of human love when it reaches out to a hurting friend, we affirm that such love is truly serving as love should. Why then must we doubt that God's love is not, from a human point of view, made all the richer because it too moves in to join the loss and hurt of our global family? Somehow such a thought seems to put a deep rich burgundy into the love of God.

I have already sat through my lifetime quota of sermons which pronounce that although God cares, He cannot experience pain and loss like people do. They declare that God sits on His throne with nothing but perfect energies flowing through Him and to Him. Now the part about God not suffering or hurting due to His own mistakes I can buy. Since He makes no errors, He certainly ought not to have to sit down to a banquet of terrible consequences. But the other part about Him not truly hurting with those who hurt and weeping with those who weep flies in the face of too many scriptures to be true. Either God has entangled himself with the human race to the point of sharing our pain, or else He is not walking what He talks.

The fact that God is perfect needs to be understood in terms of the facet of His personality being discussed. In the area of God's knowledge of human pain and suffering, His perfection does not mean that He remains untouchably distant, but that He chooses to be involved perfectly. A god who is not perfect would hardly be worth acknowledging, much less worshiping. And a perfect God who held anything less than a pure and deep concern for His creation would at best deserve a bad name.

But God does not leave the world with its citizens spinning dizzily in space with no whiff of concern. Not a single turn of the globe catches God contemplating only himself in the solitary vacuum of space. He crowds in close to the lives of people and weeps with the crying and laughs with the merry. Just as a pastor dies a little at every funeral and marries again a little at every wedding, so God identifies with the hopes and fears of all whom He has created. Martin Luther offered a delightful picture which paints God's nearness and His greatness all in one scene. "Even an humble straw," he said, "lying flat on the surface of the waters can feel the boundless power of the ocean surging through it."

God does not waste grace. He does not spend time applying His mercy where we have no need for mercy. When God offers His help, He focuses

His power at the point of need. When we stub our toe, we do not grab our thumb and nurse it, pretending that the smarting toe isn't down there. Nor does God insist on helping us with matters which don't even concern us at the moment. If we are praying about healing in an acute case of damaged memories, God does not at that moment minister to our future need for healing in a relation with a new friend. When a need emerges into clear focus, and it is our dominant need of the hour, it will in that same hour have God's help. God pinpoints His grace. He becomes a very present help in time of need. God knows what is up in our lives and if what is up merits His attention and care right away, He zeroes in on the spot. Because God resonates so closely with His creatures, He never misses an opportunity to be present at our time of searching. When with all our hearts we truly seek Him, we find that He was there all the time ready to rush all the resources of heaven to our side.

GOD'S CARE RUNS DEEP

Whenever God sets about to respond to His children's prayers, the first thing He does is to envelop the whole process in love. In fact, the very act of God's turning toward our prayers happens within a cloud of holy helping love. It never crosses God's mind not to hear our sincere prayer. There never is a split second of hesitation on His part as to whether or not He will move to meet our plea for help. If we wrestle with a question of whether God will even listen, we can be sure that such fear is prompted by Satan, because God never declines to turn an attentive ear to the call of His children.

God never has to be persuaded to care. His bias runs so heavily in our favor that efforts at persuading Him to care more are like trying to convince ice to be cold or water to be wet. Caring so belongs to His nature that even if He tried, He couldn't care more. We sometimes use the term "unconditional" to describe God's love and care. What we really mean is that with all the centuries of handling and mishandling, His care has never become shopworn or passé. Forever and a day He keeps plunging heart-forward into our concerns.

As people we care to varying degrees. Our concern is more intense when our parents are facing serious surgery or our child has been struck by a ball bat and has suffered a mild concussion. When we read in the paper of a fatal car accident or of a fatality at a construction site, we care, but nowhere near as much as when our own mother passes away.

God does not experience greater or lesser care. Because He knows everyone equally and because He cares completely, He feels exactly the same grief about every life that is lost. No obituary in our local paper slips by Him. He never passes over a single scene of woe without experiencing the infinite and complete care that He alone is capable of feeling.

Care is God's love working at our point of pain. Like the raindrops which finally saturate the soil, so God's care is the direct touch of His love on the heart of His people. For God, caring means baring His holy heart of concern for us to see and feel. When we pray, the very words we speak pour into the reservoir of God's care.

God's care reaches to more areas of our life than just our hurts. He cares with detailed awareness about the other stages of life through which we pass. God can sing more than one note. His repertoire contains our range of feelings like the ocean contains a gallon of water. John, writing from the Island of Patmos, was right. God's voice is as the sound of many waters (Rev. 1:15). The massive rising tides and the bubbling gurgle of a mountain spring are all within His range. He can care for one person going through the raging waters and at the same time be part of the joyous peace of another heart.

Certainly God's compassion runs deep. Every virtue that appears in the network of human life finds its superlative expression in God. When you discover either in your memory or in your future the highest moment of noble selfless love you can, you are observing an act which only scratches the surface of what God by His nature is eternally – compassionate love.

A second-grade teacher in Milwaukee challenged her class at the beginning of the new year to write a short article on something important they had learned during the summer. One essay stood out. The title chosen later ran: "Don't Get Perconel With a Chicken."

> On my vacation I visited with my gran parents in Iowa and my gran father learned me dont get perconel with a chicken. My gran father has a few chickens and one was a chicken I got perconel with and gave the name Gene Autry. One day my gran mother deside to have stood chicken for dinner and says Orf and you go out and kill a hen meening my gran father. I went with him and low and behole he took a pole with a wire on the end and reeched in the pen and got Gene Autry by the leg and pulled him out and before I coud say a werd he rung his neck wich pulls off his hed and he flops around on the grond back and forth without no hed on and I cryed. He was a brown one. Then he scalted him in hot water and picket the feathers of and saw my crying and

says dont ever get perconel with a chicken. When we are at the dinner table he says it again so I ate some, a drumb stick. I dident say anything but it was like eating my own rellatives. So dont get perconel with a chicken, also a cow if you are going to eat it later on. Also a caff.[2]

God got "perconel" with us. He could have spared himself the grief, but He bound himself to the human family in holy care.

Care means to move our heart into another's heart. It means to grab hold and wrestle with the agony that is dragging down a neighbor. It means absorbing into your own life part of the ache that is tearing at the heart of another. And God does that. God is no bleacher preacher. In our fight against Satan He locks arms with us in the fray and wards off the overpowering blows. So entangled does He become with us that we sometimes glimpse the stunning insight that the battle is not ours but the Lord's.

Care is of God as heat is of fire. Because of who He is, God cannot help but care. In a mystical way far beyond our mind's ability to comprehend, the heartbeat of our prayer pulses again as it moves into the heart of God. God invented prayer in order for His children to stay in touch, and because God is behind the method as well as the message, what happens by means of it matters to Him. The thesis that God can do as He pleases and that He really doesn't have to care about us may look good on paper, but it's not true in life. God has within himself decided that caring will belong to every motion of His being. His very person does not allow Him to relate to us without care. It is time wasted to speculate on what God might do. What matters is what He does do. And the eternal truth is, God has fixed care into His being so thoroughly and eternally that He can never experience carelessness, only everlasting concern.

He will never be guilty of the level of concern which one fourth-grade class had for their teacher who took sick and missed a week of school. The note which the teacher received in the mail contained only one sentence, "Your fourth-grade class wishes you a speedy recovery – by a vote of 15 to 14."

GOD GOES TO WHERE THE HURT IS

God goes to where our hurt is. He never passes by on the other side. He knows that life is bittersweet and when He sees hurt, He steps right up to rub His healing concern into the open wound. If everybody else in the world passes the need by, God's promise, through the Good Samaritan story, is that at least one, even if it has to be Christ alone, at least one person will stop by (Luke 10:30-37). In our times of pain, God always has a person standing by to care.

One of the vivid memories of my childhood which still, even in reflection, vibrates with its original feeling and color, centers around my younger brother's near brush with death. As a baby, Dan suffered from a severe adenoid condition. At age six he weighed only thirty-two pounds. At first my father resisted an operation, but finally the deterioration of Dan's breathing made the situation a matter of do or die. As a twelve-year-old boy I remember with dread standing alongside my dad and mom as the medical attendants wheeled my brother's tiny body, now anesthetized, through those screechy metal doors and down the hallway toward the operating room. Our attempts at optimism had long since melted into tears of fear.

Through my tears I could see dimly down the hall the shadowy figure of a man walking briskly toward us. Mom recognized him first. It was our pastor. Little did he realize that he was about to give our family a moment of ministry which would live in our memories forever. He walked right up to us and without ever opening his mouth, he put his long arms around all three of us – Dad and Mom and me. And he cried. Not out loud. But I looked up through that triangle of bodies above me into the eyes of my pastor and he was crying with us. I thought he looked the most like God of anyone I had ever seen. A surge of hope ran powerfully through my boyhood mind. From that divine moment, the dread began beating a retreat from my heart. A few minutes later he prayed, but the prayer could not touch what he had already spoken through his tears. God in that moment had come down in the likeness of a man.

I knew faintly then and I believe even more firmly now that closely identifying with another at his point of need may well be the most eloquent and eternal response we can ever give. When my brother left the hospital five days later, more alive than he had ever been before, I traced most of the victory to God's response to a pastor's tears.

God knows when to wall the waters up on both

sides of us. He knows when to lead us through the lowlands on dry ground. Life can crowd in upon us in a flash. But God is able to knock out a wall as easily as we might kick over an old rotten stump.

Nothing can separate us from the love and care of God.

> *Among so many, can He care*
> *Can special love be everywhere?*

Yes, by all means, yes! While life offers no asbestos to shield us from the heat and hurt of our world, neither can it keep us from being overwhelmed with the marvelous majesty of God at our place of pain. Sure, life has to be lived. And at times we must move with dizzying difficulty. God knows that there are lots of walking wounded people among us. But God also *has* to care – it's His nature. And for every person who turns strongly to Him, He continues to be a very present and powerful help in time of need. The Welsh miners knew that truth well. It was said of them that while they trudged the dull gray soils laboring for a pittance, in their souls they walked with God.

GOD KEEPS HIS VOICE DOWN

God cares enough about us to stay in close corrective touch, but it is crucial to remember that God's contacts are gentle and can be easily missed in the hubbub. The reason that it is so easy to miss God's messages is that He keeps His voice down. When a person acts unruly and disgraces His name, God never flies into a rage and screams. Nor does He scowl and stalk away mumbling, "You'll pay for this." Getting even with us through a shouting match is not God's way of proceeding. He has too much divine dignity for that.

I vividly remember that my baseball coach in high school did not take after God in this matter of voice control. I cannot remember a single practice session which managed to end without him straining both vocal cords and probably his nasal passage as well on some fairly innocent victim. A sharply hit ground ball would bounce off the shortstop's glove and Coach Busby instantly had both hands and one pair of lips flailing the air. He had one of the best collections of four-letter words around and during practice a good percentage of them got exposure. We won a game or two but most of us on the team were convinced that it had nothing to do with coach's ability to chain together bad words.

God's approach to giving advice is wholly different. Carefully built into our deepest inner selves lies the gentle voice box which God often uses to speak His helping word to us. We call it the conscience. In His design God has given that voice box of the soul two fascinating features. First, it is so quiet that another person can be standing right by your side and never hear your conscience calling at all. But on the other hand, when it is working properly, it is so loud in your own soul that you can barely drown out its noise, no matter how deafening the outside distractions. And through this silent inner messenger, God often advises and gives correction. As prayer leaves our heart, it passes by the conscience where it receives either approval as blending in with God's will or disapproval because it is running wide of it. Quietly God nudges us either to continue in prayer about a matter or else assures us that He has a better alternative in mind. Our awareness of God's hint may take a while to come clearly into focus, but if we can be patient, it will come.

There is one frightening fact hidden away in this matter of the conscience that needs regular refreshing. The Bible insists that the conscience can be muffled so long that its ability to send clear sharp messages is squelched. The very same God who allows us to choose between His will and ours will not persist in showing us His will against a steady stream of resistance. God is patient far beyond our poor power to understand that word, but even God's patience does not last forever.

The call then is to be careful that we not take the quietness of God's voice to mean that there is no authority and clout in what He is saying. Just because He does not yell out His precise intentions does not mean that He has none. It is still true that only as we keep silence before Him that the intense communication of our soul's whisper and His divine response can occur. The way of the world is to push toward a shouting match. The way of God is to speak in the low and lovely decibels of winsome love so appropriate to the small sacred privacy of our soul.

CARE CHANGES THINGS

At times in our ventures with God, our soul opens up to new vistas and in the sudden onrush of insight we feel as if we know God all over again. Less frequently we go to exciting but less reasonable limits and feel as if we all but know Him completely.

On the other hand, life often jolts us with hard-knock ruthlessness and we feel as if God has forsaken our cause. When life settles in sternly around us, jabbing and stabbing us from several sides, we rarely find anyone who can snap his fingers and banish all the irritations instantly. More often than not, the person who helps us most is not the one who glibly tells us that life will be better. Nor is it the person who tries to insist that the terrors are not nearly as frightening as they seem. The person who helps us most is the one who sits down and endures the stressful quietness with us – not jerking on the tender nerve strings of our soul, but silently sharing in the holy nearness of God.

My friend Donna served Christ in just such a situation. In a Sunday morning service in Quincy, Massachusetts, she heard what others heard – a young pastor from the midwest had been flown to Boston's Massachusetts General Hospital and needed the church's prayers. If she got a chance, Donna remembered thinking, she would drop by and tell him the church people were praying for him.

During the following week on a Tuesday evening, Donna walked into the office, looked over her roster for the night and headed down the hall. When she first looked in on Jim, lying in his hospital bed, she did not make the connection between him and the prayer request of the Sunday before. What she did quickly realize, however, was that here lay a desperately sick young man. Signs of rapid worsening already lined his face. In the chair to the side of the bed sat Jim's wife, Ellen. After only a brief moment Donna felt her heart and love bond gently to theirs. She learned that Jim and Ellen had just assumed their new pastorate but due to the sudden downturn in Jim's condition they had been forced to fly to Boston leaving their two children, ages five and seven, behind. No one knew how long or short they would need to stay.

Day after long day Donna sat with Ellen and cared for Jim. She often found Ellen sitting alone in the waiting room in the early hours of the morning crying, thinking about her children many miles across the mountains, wondering if Jim would ever return to them alive.

Then one evening as Donna arrived at work the doctor met her in the hall.

"Bad news," he said. "Jim has just died. Ellen was with him holding his hand. You may want to go down and be with her. She's alone."

Donna hurried down the hall and into the dimly-lit waiting room. Ellen was standing alone at the window looking far away into the evening sky. The sun was setting in the west.

"I'm sorry, Ellen," Donna began. "Would you like to go to my home for a couple of days before you return home? I'll be happy to take you right now."

"No," Ellen responded, "I was just thinking and praying for the children. Jim would want me to go be with them right away. He's all right now. Honestly I would like to fly back home tonight if I could. Do you think we might catch a plane tonight?"

Donna promised that she would do her best. In a couple of quick calls she learned that the last flight was leaving Boston's Logan Field for Chicago in thirty minutes. Hurriedly they threw Jim and Ellen's clothes in the suitcase, ran to the car and headed down the expressway.

"God himself must have been directing traffic on the expressway that evening," Donna said later. "It was like the Red Sea parting to allow the people to pass over on dry ground. Cars seemed to move over, lights on the off roads turned green."

And all the while Ellen sat in the passenger's seat talking of the love of God and thanking Donna for going out of her way to help.

In a few short minutes with God's miraculous help, they made the flight. As the plane roared away into the western night Donna thought to herself, "How in the world can a person have a faith in God like that? How can that young woman show such incredible strength in such a dreadful hour?"

A week later Donna received a letter from Ellen. The letter told of the funeral celebration and of a family trying to rebuild with a major building stone missing. Ellen ended with a P.S. "Oh yes, Donna, I mean to pay you for all the help you gave me just as soon as I get the money."

Donna said, "I sat down with the letter in my hands and prayed through my tears. Oh God, please give me more of the kind of beautiful faith that Ellen has. Thank You for letting her life brush next to mine for a few days. Let her know that she has already repaid me in a way that far exceeds anything I could ever have done for her."

In mutual care, both of these lives, Donna's and Ellen's, had moved miles along on their way to being more like the Master. In walking the lonely road of death, they had walked it as friends. And in a mysterious way far beyond the power of words to tell they had mounted up on wings as eagles. Together they had seen God.

CHAPTER
5

GOD ALLOWS:
Plenty of Elbow Room

GOD IS NO SNOOP

Nobody likes a snoop. Nobody I know appreciates a person infected with a nosy spirit. A prying person makes fast and furious enemies. There he goes horning in on another's private space and making himself an annoying nuisance. The whole human race hates snoopers. A snooper grates on the patience. He interferes where he has no business. And once a meddler gets going, it seems that there is no end to all the butting in on other people's concerns.

If God ever got a reputation as a snoop, He'd lose mounds of credibility overnight. If just once He decided to trample human freedom and bull His way into our freedom range, there would be accusations against Him flying all over the place. "So God's sticking His nose in where He gave us freedom to manage." Or, "What's God tryin' to do? Throw His weight around?" Or, "Where's all that freedom the Bible promised?" No, it simply wouldn't do. God's name would suffer violently if He barged in and cornered just one person or tried to force just one hand. And God knows that. That's why He has given us freedom and in spite of the inconvenience it has caused Him and the risks involved, He has stuck by His word. You won't find any sane person accusing God of being a snooper. And the reason for that is, He isn't. He conducts himself in such a way that if anybody did accuse Him of being an arm-twisting busybody, nobody would believe it.

One of the memorable things about the graduate school which I attended was the amusing fact that everybody had to share a mailbox with at least one other student. Through my entire course of study, I never did meet the person who shared my box. From the disappearance of mail, however, I continued to assume that he existed. I knew by sorting through the mail that his name was Tom Crouse. I also knew that he really lived because he would occasionally leave my half-opened mail in the slot with a note scribbled across it, "Opened by mistake. Didn't see your name until I had it open. Sorry. Tom." Funny thing was he always managed to open covert material like my semester grades or my billing notices. I had half a hunch that he was compiling a resumé of my mailbox habits to send to the FBI. Probably the rest of my mail which looked intact had been held up to the hallway light to see if any other useful data valuable to the government might be gleaned from it. Now that I think back on it, it's just as well that the two of us never met!

When it comes to respect for our private decisions, God limits His power. He doesn't even hint of nosing into our personal freedom and forcing us against our will. We can pick and choose. Even in such weighty matters as our eternal destiny, we are free. If we take wrong turns and choose to bypass His plan, God will, if asked, offer advice, but never will He pressure us into a decision we don't care to make. Nobody has ever accused God of pushing His way into their lives without permission and nobody ever will.

What if God played at this game of life with the same level of lurching inconsistency which we sometimes exhibit? What if He, like the one who planned the race in "Alice in Wonderland," set no starting point and no ending point, everyone scattering off in all directions? Happily for us, that will not occur. We may break God's rules, but He will never break them. And when God made freedom a part of the process of individual human life, He meant it. His sticking by His own rules prevents Him from yanking that freedom away from us in a flash of reaction.

The reason that this truth about freedom is so hard to fully grasp is that it runs so contrary to the human way of working. Our tendency is not only to offer advice, but to follow up with a few suggestions on how to use it. We view our calling as one of improving others.

A few years ago my cousin, Joey, and I drove deep into the hill country of Kentucky to participate in a mutual friend's wedding. We gave ourselves a couple of extra hours to find the church and wound up driving right to it and having the two hours left over. Since the town was hardly the entertainment capital of the world, we decided to drop in on the local barber for a trim. Nothing quite like a neat neck trim to give just the right touch to a wedding.

So we stopped in.

We should have noticed it right away, but we didn't. Not another soul was anywhere within earshot of that barber's pole. But we walked in innocently enough and without too much argument over who would go first, Joey stepped right up into the chair. I remember his exact words.

"Just a trim." And for two or three minutes he dozed and I thumbed through a magazine and read a story on hunting grouse. The barber wasn't much on conversation, at least not with out-of-towners and so we sat each absorbed in his own little world. After about three more restful minutes with the hum of the clippers providing a backdrop to my reading, I half heard the barber offer a suggestion.

"Your sideburns are a little long. Don't you want them clipped up a tad higher?" His voice tone sounded like he would have taken it personally if Joey had said no.

"Fine," Joey mumbled. Another minute passed before the man struck again.

"Your hair is a mite long right here on top. You probably need a little trimmed off up here too."

I didn't remember Joey having mites, so I guessed that the word had something to do with smallness.

"Go ahead, just a little," Joey agreed.

For both of us it was one of those experiences in which you sense that something sinister is happening to you but it doesn't sink in soon enough to give you a chance to dodge it. Another few moments and a couple of paragraphs further down the page, I heard Joey yelp like he had been bitten by the dog on our mail route. I looked up just in time to see him grab his head, stand straight up in the chair and stare petrified into the mirror. He looked like he had just come as close as a man can come to a full scalping and still have his head in place!

My first thought was one of delight that he had agreed to go first. In medical terms, what had happened to his head would probably constitute minor surgery. While he begrudged the barber four dollars I grabbed our coats and ran for the door. At the wedding I distinctly remember that Joey's head made short twitching motions through the whole ceremony. I guessed that the nerve endings were still smarting from the close call.

When it comes to our freedom, God takes us at our word. If we ask for only a shave that's all He gives us. In the formation of our personal futures, He abides by our decision. He never does more for us than we ask Him to do. It is one thing to offer sound advice, it is quite another to force our way beyond advice to ramming our decision down another's throat. We may catch people doing it to people, but never God doing it to people. To know so much about us and yet to yield to our decision must take an incredible amount of long temper. But God knocks and waits.

When you think about it – that God even listens to our prayers, much less responds to them – there is cause for a steady state of ecstasy. If it is true, and we believe that it is, that God possesses a super sense so sophisticated that He can bring good from every single event of life, then it is rather remarkable that He even defers to our personal opinion at all. It is like a 747 pilot listening to an eight-year-old explain why a plane needs a rudder, or a high wire expert patiently enduring a lecture on balance from a tot who is standing on a garden hose which is lying flat on the ground.

There is one important footnote. While God listens to our prayers and respects our decisions for our private lives, it is also strongly true that He does not defer to our opinion when He sets about to plan for the future flow of history. That would be as senseless as asking a three-month-old baby to carve a turkey. The result would be at best clumsy and at worst self-destructive. God would not in His higher wisdom invest such critical matters as history and heaven with us.

It is almost impossible to believe that He trusts us with such an immortal thing as our destiny, but He does. Built into each of us is the ability to make wise decisions and sound judgments. Each person with able mental faculties can pray and mean either "Thy will be done" or "my will be done." And the God who inhabits the universe and whom the heaven of heavens cannot contain accepts the decision of every single person both for time as well as for eternity.

GOD LETS US BACK OUT

How would you handle it if you had to put up with people praying for your help but who ran short on follow-through and didn't recognize and appreciate it when help came? God allows us to pray one way and then act as if we haven't the foggiest hope that He will do anything about it. We often frame our prayers fully expecting that God will spend zero energy on them. I have heard my fair share of people ask God to break in with a miracle to get the job done and then when He wants them to be His hands or feet in the task, they fall into such verbal backpedaling that God has to reassign the errand or else suspend the whole project. Praying can so easily become little more than building verbal castles in the air. The trouble with that comes when God asks us to step out the door. It would be surprising to know how much more energy-efficient our faith would be if God could get the people who pray the prayers to help set the table. When God needs a hand He tends to reach for several near the job site. God wills that men and women pray everywhere lifting up holy hands, not only to praise, but also to let Him place their hands to the task. Praying hands need to be working and willing hands.

Yet God must work with a world in which many who call Him "Lord, Lord" fail to sit down to count the cost. In my younger days there was a phrase which regularly made the rounds in our church during prayer time. It ran like this, "Oh, Lord, grant this request at any cost." At age seven, I didn't lose any sleep on the drastic, far-reaching possible implications of that line. But on later reflection I remember that a few of those who used the plea religiously dodged any assignment in the church or community which even remotely smelled of responsibility. Every election found them sitting in just the right pew to decline this or to avoid that and with no apparent thought that the phrase "at any cost" might mean them taking on a job in the church which didn't exactly fit their definition of convenient.

G. K. Chesterton once said that no truth is real until it is local. The soul-wrenching prayers which begged God's help at any price sounded good out there in the abstract, but when the vote came around and the church needed cleaning or the youth group needed leading, all the pious blather turned to pitiful backtracking. And I suspect that while God may have limited the species, not all that group will die and be buried beside my home church. Those are the kind of people that we can take only in small doses and yet God allows them to back out. He hears their sweeping promises. He listens to them make bold grandiose statements about how willing they are to give of their best to the Master. And then God, in His long-winded patience, allows them to back completely away from their claims and while it may hurt His kingdom, He loves them and goes right on. He loves people whose sporadic prayers give them only sputters of power. People who have art without heart, show without glow. God puts up with a lot. Whenever we are tempted to question His willingness to help, we must also pay attention to the other side of that coin — our willingness to follow through.

GOD LIVES WITH LOOSE ENDS

Because God is so consistent in granting us freedom, He ends up living with a lot of situations which He personally would like to see improved. The ideal world which He holds constantly before His face is forever standing in contrast to the blunt sinfulness and stark brutality which so mars our present world. And we may be sure that if God has to live with undeveloped and defaced pictures, we in our smaller worlds will have to do the same. If God has to put up with loose ends, we can go ahead and mark it on our calendars that we will need to learn to accept unresolved areas in our lives as well. Nobody relishes living with a long list of uncertainties. As far as I can tell, nobody runs around searching for insecurities to weave into the pattern of their lives. We much prefer clarity and closure. We crave for life to come to us with pharmacy-shelf neatness. And yet as long as freedom remains a generous gift from God, loose ends will live on as well.

It is a delightful day of discovery when we glimpse and grasp the insight that life is a long line of beginnings and endings – both good and bad – and that they keep coming to us in about equal proportions. Most of us come from a long line of distinguished worriers. But in God's time and way we learn to strike a balance between rock-solid certainties and nettling question marks. For every question that finds its answer, there will always be another that is still on the search. If we crave a security that is based on neat periods at the end of all of life's sentences, we will at best live with regular frustration and at worst, personal devastation. Christ simply does not answer every question; but He offers himself as the answer to every question. The one sure foothold on the landscape of life is the promised nearness of Christ. And for those of us who invite His presence, in time a number of our other questions shrink down to their proper tiny size. Others do not. There will always be questions, but the presence of Christ makes the pesky irritation of our questions not nearly so unbearable.

God has reasons for what He does. That's a fixed piece in Christian thinking. But even as we let God be God, He himself knows that He has a questioning bunch of children. As much as we trust Him, that still does not keep us from wondering what His wiser mind is up to. How is He planning to put all the pieces together? Are there any helpful insights into His ways and means of working with His people? If He does not send prompt answers to our concerns, where's the rub?

God can handle our questions. Hopefully the

days are long gone when we muzzled those who wondered out loud if God was doing all He could to help us. On life's long stressful days, the question is not only a proper one, but if it is addressed to God, it is also directed to the right Person. There are days when doubt itself is an expression of faith. When the going gets tough for us and God seems annoyingly remote, the fact that we even turn to Him reflects the truth that way down beneath our question we still believe that only God can offer answers. Our turning to God in puzzlement is still a turning to God. All along we have been taught that there is no problem too big nor too small for Him. Doubt and frustration fall in between those extremes.

To go to God even when He and His way of working are objects of our concern is still a fundamentally Christian move. With God too, honesty is the best policy. If you pray to Him in time of doubt, you will find over time that the doubt will turn over and show that it was the flip side of faith all along.

Frederich Sontag is on target, "God is not stampeded by human anxiety."[3] In our occasional pockets of anxiety, God maintains His poise and power and presence. When we find ourselves struggling for certainty and feeling that the only thing we are riveted to is change, God stands by to offer His steadying presence. We pray for peace and safety and when sudden destruction comes upon us, we strike out in search of new handholds only to discover that we are holding to God himself. When the handles become elusive, we discover a hand.

The God who sees and searches all things, even the deep things of our hearts, knows well that at times something more than earthly security is needed, and so in those times He reaches out His hand.

Bob and Karen sat in my office three days after arriving in town. Both were in their early thirties with twelve years of business success glowing behind them. They had just sold their home and traveled the 600 miles to settle in a new community with no guarantees of financial security. They only knew that God wanted them in full-time ministry and the master's program here at the school exactly suited their needs.

Bob summed up both of their feelings, "Boy, Karen and I have moved six times in the past ten years of marriage. We were hoping the constant flux was over. But here we are again. And we are convinced that God is guiding us."

Over two years I watched that couple and their three children adjust and float with the circumstances and to my delight I saw a family that had lost a great deal of the security they had back in Kansas, but who had found a zest and robust happiness that kept on growing right through the years. Sure, they would have enjoyed firm financial security, but they were more committed to a divine settledness, and for them that meant a move and less comfortable physical surroundings and more part-time jobs and less income.

We would think it foolish for a person to enter a courtroom, run up to the judge, toss him out of his chair and claim the judgeship for himself. Yet we often step to God's throne as if we might perform His task as well as He. It is against the nature of spiritual progress to try to pressure God into bringing closure to all our petitions for security. In matters of prayer and faith, the real growth comes when we learn to trust the pace of God's process in our life and in the lives of others. We do well to learn to live with a few moving targets. It is not that God wants us to look on Him as a moving wailing wall who is forever dangling answers just beyond our reach; rather He wants us to learn that growth and trust mature as we give Him our yearnings as well as our attainments.

We simply must get used to living with a few hopes which are at best strong possibilities. A few open-ended questions will continue to be a part of our lives right on through until we venture into the realm of eternity. There's no doubt that God has the power to bulldoze over everything in both His and our paths. But He allows people to use their own directional energies and as long as our freedom remains, the occasional sense of unsettledness which comes with that freedom will remain ours as well. When the boundaries refuse to emerge clear and distinct, we must let the fuzziness remain as a reminder that we are not to become fully domesticated in this world, that we seek for a city with a sure foundation whose Builder and Ruler is God (Heb. 11:10).

GOD TAKES OUR FREEDOM FOR REAL

The fact that we have more than five billion in our world means that we have the potential among ourselves to march off in a staggering number of clashing directions. Given that reality it is no small miracle that the flow of history gets along as well as it does. It is fearfully true that God has far more people around the globe who are pulling against Him than are pulling for Him. Not that God's sovereignty is up for a referendum. History is not a democracy. But God takes all His detractors seriously, which means that somewhere along the way divine hope suffers setbacks.

But nothing, not even the prayers of the noblest saint, can make God force people against their wills. The awesome gift of free will which He has given to each one of us He will never violate. Even though that fact leads to all kinds of unnecessary detours and obstructions in His divine plan, yet He honors His promise and leaves us free.

I have heard angry people ask, "Why doesn't God just go ahead and stop this nonsense of people defying His will?" "Why doesn't God just kick the silly world to pieces?" "Why doesn't God twist a few arms around here?" Questions like that deserve two or three long periods of reflection before they are answered. If God grabbed back even one person's free will and somebody found out about it, there would be nasty jibes and snowballing accusations leveled against God to such a degree that it would wind up causing nothing short of a global stink. All the claims about God being fair and impartial would be shot down for the rest of history. God's credibility as a freedom-loving and freedom-giving God would be splattered on the front page of every reputable and disreputable newspaper published in the world. People with a bone to pick with God would rise up to haunt and taunt the Christian world with ridicule about their wishy-washy God.

When life goes sour, you sometimes hear the question, "Why did God do this to me?" And while nobody should be faulted for asking a candid question, the phrasing of the question is a little misleading. It implies that God is out to get even with us at the expense of our happiness, that He is tipping the scales of fairness against us.

When Marge Hughes' husband died with cancer, her words to the pastor who visited that afternoon were, "Why did God take my husband's life?" Wisely the pastor did not that afternoon spend time explaining the fairness of God, but in later conversation with Marge, his words were well chosen.

"Marge, sin is a terrible reality which clamps its

gruesome hands on everything and every person it can find. And God hates it just like we do. Eventually He will have the last say and destroy sin with all its by-products. But in this life sin is still very much with us and we must learn to live with it and call on God to help us overcome in His power."

Sin holds a lot of sway in our world, but even sin and evil are limited by God's divine tether. The tether at times stretches to incredible limits, but never too far to be drawn back again by Him. Granted that sometimes our world system appears to be out of control, lurching from crisis to crisis. (Sometimes the fits and jerks that mark much of our personal development we tend to project onto God and see Him as also fickle and haphazard.) But what looks like God's zany handling of our world is really a testimony to the truth that God gives and keeps on giving us freedom; the real spasmodic enemy we meet is us. The little boy was right. As he peered out into the dark night through his bedroom window, he turned to his mother and said, "It's too dark to go out there without a father." That's true of adults and the real world as well.

Personal freedom is a frustratingly wonderful fact. At the same time God must hold and release us. He must listen to our prayers in one direction and watch us behave and move in the other. We flit and skitter about like waterbugs on a global pond and then gripe when God doesn't keep everything in perfect harmony, free of confusion and fear.

In his book entitled *What Shall We Wear to the Party?* Sloan Wilson brings this truth as close as our backyard.

> *The hardest part of raising children is teaching them to ride bicycles. A father can run*

beside the bicycle or stand yelling directions while the child falls. A shaky child on a bicycle for the first time needs both support and freedom. The realization that this is what the child will always need can hit hard.[4]

God is a partner in freedom with every living person. We often speak of God's freedom and human freedom as if they moved in separate realms, but we come closer to the truth if we talk of a shared freedom. God has decided to hold back voluntarily from exercising the uncut freedom of which He is capable. He has chosen instead to share His freedom with us. That means practically that in this moral universe, we the people have been gifted with an extraordinary portion of freedom which can only be described as magnificent and broad. While God owns all freedom, out of His desire to bond our love to His love, He extends to us sizable flexibility in managing our freedom as we choose. He may "carefront" us at points along the way, but He will not finally block our path.

Such wide and wonderful liberty brings with it one partner – responsibility. Freedom and responsibility are the inseparable twins of Christian stewardship. God has modeled His freedom for us. He has developed the plan of salvation and freely offers to us the possibility of receiving this plan as a personal gift. At the same time He is forever hoping and urging that we tend to our gift of freedom as dutifully and as well as He has His. It is all right to pray to God for help, but we need to remember that because of the amazing personal freedom which we possess, we are responsible for helping to answer our own prayers.

On a Monday night football telecast, Al Michaels

was reflecting on more than football when he noted, "A football team does not have an endless number of chances to score in a game. Maybe twelve or thirteen at most. And each time a team loses the ball, it loses one of its few precious opportunities to score."

Responsibility is in our hands and we dare not squander the grand privilege we have to turn it to our good. From His side, God softens people's hearts, for example, to receive the gospel. But from our side we are responsible for making sure that the gospel seed is planted in the fertile heart. From His side, He takes responsibility for forgiving us when we have offended a friend with harsh words. But in our freedom we are responsible for adding a word of apology for our mistake. The fact that God takes our freedom seriously means that a lot more of the responsibility for seeing things come to pass belongs to us than we are used to admitting. When Christ urged us to occupy until He came, He meant that we were to enjoy and employ the roomy freedom in which we live and play to see that His kingdom goes divinely forward, sitting partly on our shoulders.

CHAPTER
6

GOD PLANS:
Sticking To the Outline

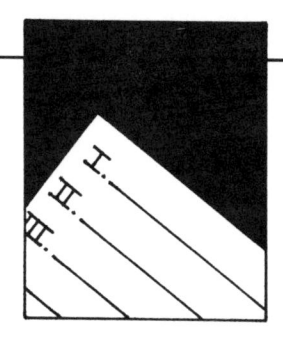

GOD WORKS WITH A WELTER OF MOTIVES

In my childhood neighborhood, a half dozen of us boys formed a club which we named, or more correctly misnamed, The Flying Squadron. The title was faulty on two counts. As far as I can remember, none of the airplanes we built ever flew, and second, we found the "squadron" on the side of a kitted airplane box and thought it had a mystical connection with flying so we adopted it. We would have struck closer to reality if we had called ourselves, The Trial and Glaring Error Modelers. We would buy up three or four plastic airplane kits and then converge on our backyard shop for a mass construction project. Most of the airplanes ended up being design mixtures – any single plane being a prototype by assortment. If we misplaced the landing gear from one kit we would adapt the same from another one. About the only thing Orville and Wilbur would have appreciated would have been our creativity.

What kept the assembly sessions from being pure exercises in futility was that wonderful invention called the Exploded View. As often as we could, we purchased kits which had the small red oval on the box lid which read "Exploded View inside." That meant that inside the kit lay a picture plan for assembling all the pieces to the main body of the airplane. Little dotted lines zigzagged here and there to show where wheel pants should be connected and Pitot tubes inserted and tail fins slotted. Once in a while we would stick to the letter of the layout and a sleek scale-like model would take shape before our eyes. We usually painted the ones that made it to the fully assembled stage.

Unfortunately, with diverse people and cultures and nations, life is so complex that no one can even sort out all the motives in order to give us a simplified exploded view. We may pray as if God could look down from heaven and sort through all the motives and motions and group people into neat piles, condemning Group A and rewarding Group B and making justice an instant reality. But that would be an exercise in simple mindedness. It would be one more case of the clay saying to the potter, "Here is the defective clay, please remove it now." God moves forward amid an incredibly complex tangle of motives and free wills. No exploded view reduces His task to a few simple insertions and removals.

Sometimes in managing His world, God's larger plans may cut across and foil our plans. But if we are committed to His sovereign will, our foil is our gain. Elmer Duncan, in his work on Sören Kierkegaard, mentions the preacher who once gave a sermon at a university chapel. The subject was missions and the invitation at the end of the sermon asked, "Who will go for Christ? Who will take the message of Christ to the steaming, disease-ridden jungles of Africa? Who will seek out the persons who have never heard the story of the Savior? Who will go to those dying in darkness?" The preacher paused for emphasis and the silence was broken by soft but distinct words, "I'll go, Father, I'll go." It was the minister's daughter, his only child. The preacher was so shocked that he blurted out, "No, not you." But the little girl insisted, "Yes, I need to go." In time she did.[5]

If we ask God to shine on the just and rain on the unjust, we are really asking Him to do the equivalent of writing a full-length true-to-life novel using only twenty-five vocabulary words. We rush in far too quickly with handy and ready solutions to problems which must seem to God like trying to prop up the Brooklyn Bridge with toothpicks. Our thoughts simply do not move at the level of His thoughts. Our ways easily crowd and complicate His own.

The human brain has a unique ability which gets its share of misuse. It has the capacity to imagine vivid concrete realities which God does not get particularly excited about. And yet when God plans, His plans include our plans. Amid all the swirl of tiny human plans, He plans. When we have laid out our dispensation charts and plotted nearly every last event of history's conclusion down to the nearest minute, God scans His larger more encompassing plan and accepts our honest tries at helping Him. But make no mistake, God's job is never as simple as it may appear. Our easy solutions have more to do with the limitations of our view than with the ability of our God. Grappling as He does with multiple motives, God must deal with such a staggering array of variables that to even glimpse His sovereign assignment would instantly overwhelm us. He must at times have to smudge out the borderlines which we have drawn too narrowly and push farther out to find His answers. We would probably do ourselves a great favor to stand again amazed at how much God can bring out right when we consider the jumble with which He has to work.

We put words in His mouth and then claim to be quoting Him. The late E. W. Black related how his seven-year-old, Melvin, came rushing into the house one day and said, "There's a lion in our backyard. Come, Daddy, look at this lion."

"Now, son, you know better than that. There is no lion in our backyard. Not in Asheville, North Carolina. It's probably just a neighbor's dog."

"No, Daddy, I just saw it. There's a lion out here." The little boy was persistent, so after hearing the line repeated a half dozen times. E. W. decided to go out into the yard and settle the score. "Okay, let's go see it." He walked out of his office and around the house and there standing in the middle of the yard was a huge brown shaggy dog. The little boy's eyes lit up.

"There it is, Dad, there it is!"

"Son, listen, you know that's not a lion, that's just a dog and I want you to tell Jesus you're sorry. I want you to go in the house and ask Him to forgive you for acting like that was a lion."

Melvin hurried off to his room and in a minute he was back. "Did you tell Jesus you were sorry?"

"Yes. I told Him I was sorry, but He said the first time He saw it He thought it was a lion too!"

What fun God must have when we speak for Him.

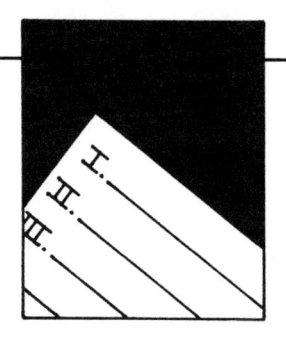

GOD HELPS THE PIECES TO FIT

A lot of what happens to us in life doesn't at first seem to fit. Sometimes for things to blend in with life, we have to lengthen and broaden our view. In a moment of shortsightedness, we can focus in on one awkward ill-fitting part and end up doubting if the piece is useful at all.

Take Joseph. No doubt when he first began bumping around in that cart headed for bondage in Egypt, he prayed a good many prayers for prompt release.

"At least let the camel stumble, oh God, or let the cart break open so I can make a run for it."

In Potiphar's home, he must have prayed often for release from the powerful temptation with which the woman taunted him. It was quite an insight when Joseph finally realized that all his predicaments were intended by others for evil but God meant them for good. If God had answered all of Joseph's prayers along the way, there would probably be no story of famine and grain and God's deliverance as we read it in the Bible. But God was planning ahead and Joseph's prayers for God to use him in the best way possible were in the long run the ones God rightly chose to answer. At points along the way the taste must have been bitter, the smell putrid. But God knew exactly the dosage of trials to administer to Joseph so as to prepare him for the greater challenges which lay ahead.

My brother and I used to enjoy the challenge of a good jigsaw puzzle. On a rainy Saturday afternoon, after thirty minutes each before a boring metronome and John Thompson's piano lesson books, we'd dump a thousand-piece puzzle on the dining room table and there went the rest of our day. Other people probably have never experienced it. But in our adventures with jigsaw puzzles, we almost always had a dozen or so pieces which we would vow, with our hands raised to heaven, had gotten into our box by mistake. There never was, nor would there ever be, a place for such odd and ugly pieces. No color that shade even appeared in the pretty picture on the cover of the box.

And then we would get near the end of the puzzle and all at once those pieces fit like magic and we'd smile at our earlier plan of calling up Milton Bradley to see if they wanted us to send back the dozen extra pieces from our box. Perhaps they would want to send them to the rightful owner. But on all the occasions I can remember, Milton Bradley had gotten just the right number of pieces in just the right box and to our regular chagrin, they all finally fit.

Life goes together a lot like that. If you haven't had a day or two that you would declare had served no useful purpose, look out, it's coming. Once in a while you will strike a real loser of a day with why-did-I-get-up written all across it. How in the name of reason, you will say, did such a day ever get in my box? Somebody surely must be playing a cruel practical joke on me. But before you send it back, hang onto it for a later look. It may well be that segments of life which look like they are about as useless as a flyswatter at the North Pole are really quite important to the puzzle. Finally, when all is over, part of life takes longer to show its purpose and place than other parts. Some lessons flow easily. Others take lots more time and thought and trust; the mind absorbs them more slowly. But once they start to fit, the puzzle takes another step toward completion and the full beauty of life with all of its darker and lighter tones comes more clearly into view.

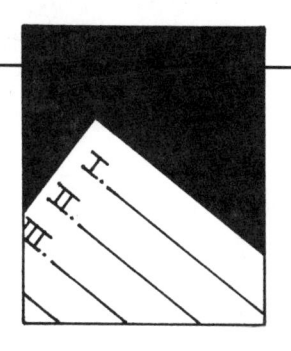

GOD MAKES THE ROUNDABOUT WAY HIS WAY

One of our most human tendencies is to want to correct a person who makes a mistake right away. If a person missteps, we want to reach out and jerk the person back into line and save God the trouble. The problem with that is, when we try, without being told, to help God as He helps others, we create resistance in the person and tension in our relationship with him. Instead of us changing people, we must keep letting God do the changing.

A turn of phrase that points out the folly of forcing others against their wills says it well, "A man convinced against his will is of the same opinion still." It is a lesson which comes slow in the learning that God's persuasion gets longer-lasting results than does ours. God's way of improving persons may not happen with nearly the speed we would like to see, but the way He works wears better over time. His way of working deserves a second look. Our desire to instantly correct may look good on paper, but going through God in prayer, taking the roundabout way, brings more enduring change.

Dennis Kinlaw put exactly the right words in exactly the right way when he noted, "Give me one divine moment when God acts and I say that moment is far superior to all the human efforts of man throughout the centuries."[6] Prayer often seems such a slow way to proceed. Far better to jump in and command a wayward person's repentance than to wait around for God's stubborn love to melt down the resistance. But time after time people who were backsliding in spirit have only been pressed into more rapid regression by cold confronting when they might have been better served by prayerful carefronting.

Recently a couple asked me to provide marriage counseling for their twenty-year-old daughter and her prospective bridegroom. The letter asking my help contained chilling words:

> This girl has broken mine and her mother's heart. We have just discovered that she has already been living with this man to whom she is not married. Her mother and I have insisted that she see you before she can even return home. If she marries this man, at least we will have the consolation that she is equally yoked together with an unbeliever.

A follow-up phone call to the parents revealed that they had shut the daughter out of their home until she "cleaned up her life." Solving problems, especially mammoth ones like this, is rarely done by a head-on collision of wills. The far superior way is to pass the responsibility over to God through prayer to seek His miracle of conflict resolution long before the tension reaches the white-hot heat of rage and rebellion. Coercion is the lowest form of persuasion and almost never works. But if we can pray and then stand back long enough to watch God work, we will find better reward for our labor. It is almost never the easiest way, but in the end, we may well find that the roundabout way was the divine way.

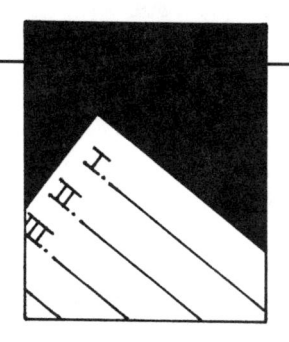

GOD NEVER SECOND-GUESSES HIMSELF

Unlike us, God never second-guesses himself. Since He decides exactly right the first time, any other option, even if He considered it, would at best be second best. From the foundation of the world God decided to send His Son to save the world and at no point along the way did He quibble with that decision. Clearly that was the toughest decision God ever made. But even in that divine dilemma, He made a choice in our favor and stood by it.

He had ample time to reconsider. From the start of creation to the announcement by Gabriel to Mary was quite a stretch. But instead of divine doubts being dropped along the way, we see in holy history a steady stream of hints that God was holding firm to His position – for our salvation a sword would pierce His Son's side. God never entered into a running debate with himself about an alternate plan. The pages of revelation do not contain a single sentence of suspicion on the part of God that what He had planned from the beginning might be the figment of a misguided divine mind. Sure, the pages of the New Testament are written in the brilliant afterglow of the Resurrection. But even before the Resurrection, God was already committed to His plan for our future.

Second-guessing is strictly a human activity. And even then, we really do more of it than we ought to. Often in the tiniest turns of life we stand on our feet and vow never to change our minds. Signed, sealed and settled. And within the hour we are looking back over our shoulder and scratching our heads.

My friend Gary suffered the second-guessing illness when he first met Mary. No doubt about it, Mary was gorgeous. Every round of college publicity shots and there she was dolling up the pages and supposedly drawing in throngs of other students. New buildings and spiral stairwells looked even more appealing when she stood next to them reading a book. Plus she was good. No beast behind that beauty! Her gentle voice oozed optimism and care. She taught the seventh-grade Sunday school class. She had won the Young Christian Scholar award in her local church. She had also led a church youth fund raiser which brought in two thousand dollars to build an outdoor basketball court. But Gary was still suspicious. Even after he had taken her out and seen her for himself up close, he still agonized over how a girl could be so good and so lovely all at the same time.

"Somewhere, sometime along the way," he would say, "she's going to show a fatal flaw and then there I'll be stuck with a pretty dud."

For a while, I even helped him look for a flaw. But we couldn't find anything. We even tried thinking up flaws to look for and still she proved to be twenty-four carat, sparkling, sterling and solid. But Gary, born as he was with a question mark for a mind, could never shake his senses into believing what he was seeing. So I married her! As the years passed, Gary and I returned to a speaking and even a laughing relationship about his long string of successful second-guessing. And he has now lived long enough to have completely discarded his doubts about Mary's genuineness. Thankfully for me, it's too late.

James says that with God, there is never a loss due to His indecision. With God there is no shadow of turning, no second-guessing (James 1:17). The truth is, God never needs to turn. His far-reaching mind grooves in the perfect direction at the beginning so that no turn or sleight of hand is needed. He knows when to trust and whom to trust for He knows what is in the heart of all people (John 2:25). God's complete honesty with us is based on the pure inner integrity of His own thoughts. Since He never needs to change His mind, He never runs into a problem of explaining to us His new direction. That is why it is an error to say that God thought up the New Testament because the Old was not helping as much as He had hoped. No, the New Testament is not a change of direction from the Old. It is the widening and deepening of thoughts which God had planted earlier in seed form. Augustine was right:

> *The New is in the Old contained,*
> *The Old is in the New explained.*

God thinks ahead so far and so well that no event either in time or in eternity will ever catch Him off guard. We can bank our faith and trust our prayers to a God like that, a God who never guesses at what He is doing and therefore never needs to second-guess himself. When it comes to God, His first plan and the right plan are always the same.

CHAPTER 7

GOD HELPS:
Doing a World of Good

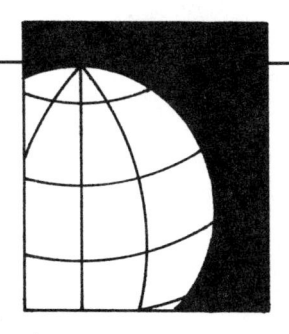

GOD PUTS GLORY ON OUR GUM

Into every life there comes a few full-fledged tumbledown days. If the sink isn't leaking, the faucet won't work. And if the strawberries won't wait another day, the market is out of freezer bags. Back-to-back blowouts. On days like that you feel like you have gone down with everything but the Titanic! To even get a prayer ready on a day like that almost requires a breakdown in the trouble sequence. To really get going with a prayer at least one thing has to go right. A breathing space has to come along.

Then in the nick of trouble-free time, when you have a second to spare, you might start with a hallelujah. Not a loud one, unless, of course, you are into decibels. But a hushed little hallelujah to let God know that you are still a long way from the chug-a-lug third time down. As my friend Betty would say when the day had been especially helter-skelter, "Well, praise the Lord anyhow!"

Very few things rank in beauty and charm with a glory moment in the middle of a day when God slips in a wedge of His grace that exactly custom-fits the hole. When life seems awfully horizontal, flooded with mostly human shortcomings, God comes alongside and clips the horizontal just long enough to assure us that there is a higher view, that heaven is waiting in the wings. God steps up and snips our string of struggle as easily as a child might blow the seeds from a fluffy dandelion.

God's involvement may not always be exactly what we were expecting, but we can be sure it is always the best thing that could happen to us. Our response to God's help may be like that of the little boy who decided to visit his dentist for a trick or treat on Halloween night. As he was backing away from the steps he peeked into his pumpkin to see what the dentist had dropped in. Right on top lay a pack of sugar-free gum. The dentist overheard his comment, "Well, you might have known." With God we can guess ahead that whatever He sends our way is going to be better for us than anything we might have picked by ourselves.

If God ever stopped entangling himself with us, our world would be one miserable crawling mass of hate and hell. Our frustration with rotten injustices and wrenching calamities would, except for the grace of God, boil much hotter. What we need to keep replaying on the screen of our minds is that because God doles out a lot of His glory and grace, this world is a much better place in which to live and move and have our being.

As rowdy boys growing up in a country church, my friend Dave and I were never able to brag, with a clear conscience, that our church attendance was employed in the ennobling art of worship. Our prankish side kept barging in on our sacred side, even in the solemn assembly. Far and away too many of our church hours were consumed scouting for splotches of fresh sticky gum under the back eight or ten pews. During prayer while others were kneeling we'd sometimes lie on our backs and scan the underside of pews hoping to spot a freshly planted wad of chewing gum to add to our collection neatly grouped under the last pew. When we found one, one of us would monitor the nearest group of adults to make sure they were safely distracted by the prayer while the other would creep and crawl to the prize and retrieve it with a slice of cardboard. Not the most sanitary of hobbies, but then we had not yet taken "Health and P.E." from Mrs. Evans, so we were innocent about deadly bacteria.

No one could have convinced us in those days that we were missing a good deal of God's glory by going for the gum. We were letting a wad of chewing gum keep us from enjoying much of the warm love which the people had for God and He had for them.

The parable of the gum holds an index finger in our direction. Sure, the days of our lives are often splotched with shame and embarrassment. Smudges of pain lie about us in almost every face we see. No person with a working piece of gray matter can deny that. But if we let ourselves get overly absorbed with looking for the gum, we too can miss the glory. God's present help can be missed completely if we are out looking for the wrong thing in the other direction. Undoubtedly we overlook a sizable amount of God's activity because we have eyes that see not and ears that hear not. The gum so rivets our gaze that large swaths of resplendent glory go unseen.

On an early morning flight from Boston to New York, I sat across the aisle from a man who kept complaining to the stewardess about the temperature of his coffee. As far as I could determine, there was for him no perfect coffee except the cup he didn't presently have. No temperature pleased him. One cup was too cold. The next was too hot. And every time he sampled the new cup, he underwent a mild tantrum. The saddest part of the scene lay in the fact that behind the man out the window of the plane, God was opening His pastels and painting one super fabulous backdrop for the New York harbor — and the man never saw it. The open furnace of the sun was all ready to blaze into view, but the man never turned his head in that direction. If only he had looked in the other direction, he could have savored the bursting beauty of the morning and let his grumbling about the cup of coffee dwindle down to a sigh. No doubt the man had left home that morning wishing his day would go well, but if it had, he would have missed it.

God's glory is easy like that to overlook. Even though health and beauty and joy may be thrilling the air around us, we so easily focus in on one ugly spot and miss the glory for the gum. Do you suppose that God sometimes has a response to our prayers all packaged and ready to go but He has to hold the delivery because we are out, absorbed to distraction by a lesser matter? The day of our visitation is right upon us, a rush of heaven is pending in our hearts, and we're looking in the waste basket for discarded gum.

There's a funny quirk in us which finds us looking for a spider web in a room full of hand-carved antiques. Or we watch an Olympic-quality ice skating performance on TV and the first thing we tell another person entering the room is about the skater's momentary slip while recovering from the flamingo. Something there is in us which sees the five-inch-long scratch and misses the perfect reflection in the rest of the mirror.

When it comes to God responding to our prayers, this same mood for seeing the motes can creep in. Without even meaning to, we catch ourselves wondering about our eggs when freshly hatched chickens are running all around us. We keep looking back to see what hasn't happened when a world full of answered prayer is teeming with life at our feet.

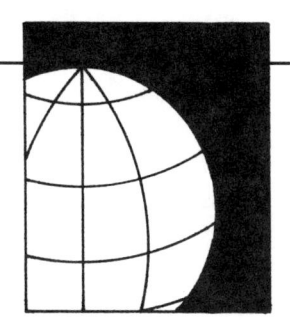

GOD GIVES SPECIFIC ANSWERS TO GENERAL PRAYERS

Recently my friend Jim visited Minneapolis on a business venture. His wife and son, Debbie and Andrew, stayed home. One afternoon Deb and Andy were in the local mall when they met a friend who turned to the two-year-old and asked,

"Andrew, where is your father?"

To which the little boy replied, "He's in Many Applesauce."

God must answer a lot of our prayers forwarded to Him when we are not real sure exactly what we are asking for. Our meaning mismatches our words. We never did bring our prayer out of the fuzzy stage before we offered it to God. Sometimes God helps us when we have prayed what would probably be better described as one oblong blur.

We're a lot like that little boy in the choir who

got off to the wrong start on his Christmas chorus. At full power he belted it out, "While shepherds washed their socks by night." And God must on occasion have to take our words which wander aimlessly in mid-air and plant them alongside a specific need and then answer them.

God does amazingly specific things for us when we remember how generally we pray. "Bless our world tonight," we pray. And God takes a sprawling line like that and answers it in behalf of a group of people ravaged by hunger or war. "Help my family, dear God." Then unknown to us, He visits an aunt who is suffering from depression and lifts her heart back toward heaven and wellness. What a God we have who can take a prayer wide enough to house the whole world in one phrase and set in motion a marvelous series of energies which meet special needs in several local places. We have to be careful before we ask God for something. He may overhear our intention and get on with the answer.

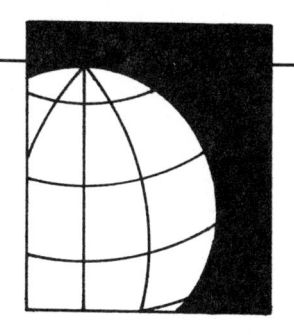

GOD WATCHES HIS SECOND HAND

Never in the history of humanity has God ever been a minute slow or fast in answering a prayer. Over six thousand years have ticked off the clock since Adam and Eve walked with God in the cool of the garden and not once from that time to this has His timing been off.

Even as Jesus groaned, "My God, my God, why have you forsaken me?" God was standing in the wings watching His eternal second hand. In His piercing pain Jesus must have wondered if God's watch had run down or stopped; if somewhere there had been a mistake; if heaven's signals had gotten crossed. But God was keeping tabs on the time and when the fullness of time was come, God the Father signaled to His Son and Christ breathed out His final life-saving breath. For four thousand years the human race had been looking for its Savior and finally in time's fullness, He had come and lived and died.

In spite of the fact that we know that we are dealing with a God for whom a day is as a thousand years, we still struggle with periods in which His work seems awfully slow. For God and for us His help "right early" may mean two different things. For Him it means in the ideal time, for us it usually means by morning.

In the interest of speed people will sometimes cut corners. But God will not, either for speed or for greed, do an inferior job. Meeting our timetable is not His primary concern. He thinks before He inks. Many of our prayers are potential bombshells. Many are headlines waiting to happen. And many of them are just plain ill-timed and bad. And God must sort through all the signals and discover the right kind of way and the right time of day to offer His help to our concern. It would do most of us a heap of good if we would just quit our quibbling and turn up our trust. How big is God anyway? If He were just great enough to have marginal power to help us, we could justify a little more worry. But God is not living at the upper edge of His power output. Energy is no problem with Him. When the Bible says that He has all power in heaven and on earth, that's a load of power. And what's more, He's ready to send more of it our way.

For many people, money matters seem to figure large in the regular list of needs. If we are going through a time of financial squeeze, we may view the crisis as a clear instance deserving God's prompt forwarding of funds. But God may view it as a time for deepening faith more than a time for funneling moneys. In His larger and longer range of thinking,

God prefers to foster faith while our hearts are turned to Him in time of need. If God believes it best, in just the nick of time money will come, but the sluggish or rapid flow of cash is neither a sign of God's favor nor lack of it. God is interested in more things than money. And His help in the greater growth patterns of life can make more dollars for the sake of dollars look terribly trivial in the long run.

God keeps working at making every situation of life, whether enjoyable or sad, contribute to our eternal well-being. His farsighted love will allow us to pass through pain and loss if He sees that these will increase our future joy. Nothing God allows to come upon us will last too long nor be unnecessary. Not a single moment of unhelpful hurt will come upon us. Somewhere, somehow He will work all things together for our good (Rom. 8:28). It is for us to keep believing with confidence that He will meet us in the right moment of time with a miracle matched to our need. True, He may stretch our patience, but even stretched patience is a side-benefit on the way to answered prayer. We may trust God with His watch. Since He invented time, we may be sure that He will always manage it to our fullest advantage.

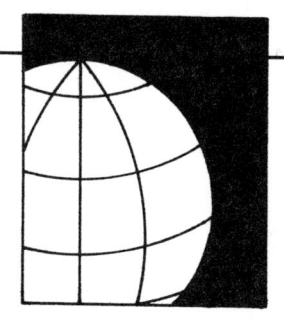

GOD PREFERS THE BACKDOOR

In a society spellbound by celebrities, we have a pesky habit of expecting all important events to start at the main entrance, to continue front and center and to end with one standing ovation after another. And while God will one day wind up being All in All, the central Person of the centuries, He almost never starts grandly. His greatest productions both on a large global scale and on the smaller personal scale start out surprisingly small. By way of beginnings, God loves a backdoor.

When Christ visited from heaven, the world was at the ready. Rumors were flying all over in the Near East that the Jewish nation represented by the constellation Pisces was due a new king. Wise men in Palestine had been collecting messianic signals from their scriptures and for them too the time was ripe.

Routinely on the streets the people talked about a star to rise out of Jacob, a sceptre out of Israel. This new leader, it was whispered, would galvanize the military muscle of the countryside. Pockets of guerilla resistance once led by the Maccabeans would soon be merged into one destructive mass of murder. All eyes were on the army. Where was this might-wielding Messiah? Was he already somewhere standing sentinel, filling his mind with strategies and maneuvers? Perhaps he was growing up in a small town like Nazareth, a little village overlooking the Valley of Armageddon. Nobody knew exactly from where he would march. But that he would emerge from the mighty military almost everyone agreed. And in the daily prayers on the lips of the people, they pled that his coming would be swift.

If messengers had scurried to all the major military posts and royal palaces on the night that Christ was born and had announced that the Messiah had just been born in a haymow, the mocking laughter would have echoed all through the next morning's news. This was no time for God to be playing jokes on His people. No time for teasing. Too many prayers had been prayed. Expectancy was running too high. The party had been too well planned for the main guest to show up dressed in poverty with lowbrow parents and a homely look.

The trouble was, in all the hoopla, the people had overlooked a divine rule of thumb. Sometimes God gets His greatest tasks off to a micro beginning. His best gifts come wrapped in the smallest packages. Usually God takes the gradual way to greatness.

So in prayer. If we rehearse the way God has taken in our lives, we will be surprised again and again at how His most sizable tasks began so unassumingly small. The number of times that God answers our prayers with an instant and full-blown response is quite rare. More often He develops a response to our prayer after He has gently walked in the backdoor. Without overwhelming us at the start, He shows us His warm accepting side and only then does He pray that we may one day be with Him that we may behold His impressive and spectacular glory.

For Bob, God came that way – gently and humbly. Bob Strand grew up in a ghetto of Chicago. His father shirked family responsibilities and disappeared from home when Bob was three. His mother, Lois, tried to keep Christ and the church as the centerpiece of the home, but as Bob grew into his teen years the pull of sin finally snapped his half-hearted commitment to the church. By age fourteen, Bob's daily routine included foraging in supermarket waste bins for scrap food and huddling in cardboard boxes warmed by factory smokestacks. By age fifteen Bob had lost track of his mother and she of him.

One night in despair and hungry to nausea, Bob stumbled into a mission house and begged for a piece of bread. He received instead a bowl of soup, a piece of chocolate cake and a long loving hug. Not since his days around his mother's apron had he been given such a needed embrace. It had been so long, in fact, that he had difficulty accepting it again. Over the year the mission staff kept an eye on Bob, the street boy. They invited him to one activity after another. One night after a roller-skating party the leader talked about a Savior who came to help street people, and Bob remembered his mother's Christ. The winsome Christian living of the mission team brought him again to a place of commitment. That night he decided that he would try once again to live for Jesus.

For the first few months after his new commitment to Christ, Bob traveled the zigzagged spiritual path that marks so many young believers. After three months he was adopted by a family only to revert to stealing and even ripping off valuable items from the adoptive family's home. Again he turned to the mission and again he set his heart to live better. He could not help but hear the verse which the staff pumped into his mind every day. "He who has begun a good work in you will continue it until the day of Jesus Christ" (Phil. 1:6). So Bob kept turning to God for help and hope. He moved into the mission and began ministering to other street people.

A few months ago I slipped into the back pew of a local Methodist church and sat down. The sign on the bulletin board outside simply read, "Evening Service: Bob Strand, Former Street Boy." When Bob stood behind the pulpit that night, neatly dressed, with his Bible and a smile, I knew again that God lives to redeem people. His sermon, which ran more along the lines of a testimony, wasn't eloquent, but at the end when the congregation rose in a standing ovation to Bob's Christ, I said again in my heart what I had heard Bob say a dozen times, "He who has begun a good work will continue it until the day of Jesus Christ." I knew in a higher and holier way than ever before that God's way in Bob's life had begun quietly, gently around his mother's Bible and would certainly continue. Martin Luther had somewhere written words which seemed suited to the occasion, "How quietly and simply do those events take place on earth that are so heralded in heaven." After the service I shook Bob's hand and hugged him. I thought as I drove home, "Even if Christ did nothing but redeem street boys and girls,

He'd still qualify as divine. But boy, does He ever do more!"

GOD IS WORKING IN THE MEANTIME

An unthinking person once said to Helen Keller, "Isn't it awful to be blind?" To which she replied, "Not half as bad as having two good eyes and never seeing anything."[7] As people of faith we must reaffirm to our hearts the truth that God is helping all the time. If we can keep on shaking ourselves awake to the subtle but certain movement of His creative hand in the world, we will discover that like concentric circles radiating in a pond, God's help is so commonplace that it may well be more difficult to find where He is not working than where He is. We may discover that while we were looking around to see the trace of His divine pen on the pages of our lives, He was holding our hand all the while, helping us write straight, using crooked lines.

If you catch yourself struggling with the question of where God is and why it seems He's not helping, look around. Every Christian you meet is an answered prayer. Every clean clear breath you draw testifies that God wanted to answer your prayer for life and health. Every time you stop your car after a long or short trip, God has once again provided the safety you talked to Him about. It is by His mercies that we are not consumed (Lam. 3:22). While we are resting, God is working. Sometimes we need to sit down on a mental cactus couch to prick our memory regarding the steadiness of His mercies.

In between high days of excitement, we ask God to bless us and He takes a generic prayer like that and sets our garden aflame with flowers and explodes the meadow with blossoms and grain. Using a little prayer like "Help us," He interprets it broadly, includes our non-Christian friends, and fills their wells along with ours with streams of living water.

Most of the marvels which figure so regularly into our daily lives come about because God is always working. For millenia He has been clustering veins of coal and pockets of oil so that dropping a shaft and drilling a well could be worth it. Each day He swirls enough freshness into the wind wrap of our world to clean this cover in which we live and breathe. He leaves electricity lying all around and then gives us the skills to put it in wires to work for us. He has stored mammoth reserves of power in the ocean tides and is still patiently waiting for us to harness it. He keeps His big magnet of gravity pulling. He grows new forests to replace burnouts. He packages love in baby-size bundles. He positions stars to play at the game of light-years. He washes the world's water in blue bubbling mountain streams. He forms building blocks strong enough to stack over one hundred stories high and hangs perfect color-coordinated pictures on the wall of the sky everyday. He builds Sahara-size sandboxes and rock mounds like the Alps for our adventure and variety. He creates delicate green vegetation on the jungle floor which He alone will ever see and enjoy. He carves tunnels in our souls so that His peace may flow between and around our pain.

We forget these assignments which God does in the meantime, but a moment's reflection on them and their size causes us to be awed by what God does in His off time. There is no such thing as God getting back to work. By Him all things cohere (Col. 1:17). Just because He is not attending to our need does not mean that He is not attending us. By Him all things hold together. Since that is true, then God must be always in the act of holding and helping. It is so easy for us when we think about God and His work to spend more time asking where He is than praising Him for where He's been. We spend time looking for places where He is apparently absent rather than rejoicing in the events at which He is obviously present.

In part this is understandable. One of the side effects of sin is that we suffer the monotony of the routine. We become jaded to any stimulus which persists too long. People who move alongside a railroad track say that for the first few months they hear every locomotive that lumbers down the line. But in time the house can rattle and the windows vibrate and the very same person that once heard every train has to be told that a train is passing by. As hard as I find it to believe, people who live near nose-burning papermills say the same is true for them. In a few months what to the rest of us who drive by is still a nauseating stench is for them just one more cloud of atmosphere on the horizon.

When it comes to God and what He does for us, we enjoy it so regularly and routinely that we phase into a degree of unawareness. Not that we mean to. It's just part of the human process. Now and then we have to give ourselves a real jolt to sensitize our souls again to the work of God. But we may be confident that our lack of awareness does not diminish God's help, because His help is not based on our knowledge of what He is doing. He keeps working in front of as well as behind the scenes. Even in our duller moments, the God who never dozes is still vividly alive to the detail of our lives working all things together for our good.

Endnotes

Chapter 1

[1] Robert Lacey, *Ford: The Men and the Machine* (New York: Ballantine Books, 1986), p. 102.

Chapter 4

[2] J. A. Battle and Robert L. Shannon, *The New Idea in Education* (New York: Harper & Row, Publishers, 1968), p. 108.

Chapter 5

[3] Frederick Sontag, *What Can God Do?* (Nashville: Abingdon, 1979), p. 28.

[4] Sloan Wilson, *What Shall We Wear to This Party?* (New York: Arbor House, 1976), p. 441.

Chapter 6

[5] Bob Patterson, gen. ed. *Makers of the Modern Theological Mind*, 10 vols. (Waco: Word Books, 1976), vol. 9: *Soren Kierkegaard*, by Elmer Duncan, p. 92.

[6] Robert E. Coleman, ed., *One Divine Moment* (Old Tappan, N.J.: Fleming H. Revell Company, 1970), p. 5.

Chapter 7

[7] Charles Allen, *Life More Abundant* (Old Tappan, N.J.: F. H. Revell Co., 1968), p. 110.